CEO Succession

CEO Succession

Dennis C. Carey
Dayton Ogden

with Judith A. Roland

OXFORD
UNIVERSITY PRESS
2000

OXFORD
UNIVERSITY PRESS

Oxford   New York

Athens   Auckland   Bangkok   Bogotá   Buenos Aires
Calcutta   Cape Town   Chennai   Dar es Salaam   Delhi
Florence   Hong Kong   Istanbul   Karachi   Kuala Lumpur
Madrid   Melbourne   Mexico City   Mumbai   Nairobi
Paris   São Paulo   Singapore   Taipei   Tokyo   Toronto   Warsaw

and associated companies in
Berlin   Ibadan

Copyright © 2000 by Oxford University Press

Published by Oxford University Press, Inc.
198 Madison Avenue, New York, New York 10016

Oxford is a registered trademark of Oxford University Press

Library of Congress Cataloging-in-Publication Data
Carey, Dennis (Dennis C.)
CEO Succession / Dennis Carey, Dayton Ogden ; with Judith A. Roland
p. cm.
Includes bibliographical references and index.
ISBN 0-19-512713-7 (alk. paper)
1. Executive succession—United States. 2. Directors of corporations—United States. 3.
Industrial management—United States. I. Ogden, Dayton. II. Title.

HD38.25.U6 C37 2000
658.4'07128—dc21   00-020412

1 3 5 7 9 8 6 4 2

Printed in the United States of America
on acid-free paper

Contents

———

Foreword

———

John A. Byrne, Senior Writer, *Business Week*

People are the lifeblood of every organization. In every corporate enterprise, in every nonprofit group, they form the communities that determine whether an organization succeeds or fails, whether they change the way we think and work or are merely superfluous to our economy and our society. That is why there are few management issues of greater importance to companies, their investors, or their employees than who will lead an organization in the future.

The book you hold in your hands not only provides welcome insight into how the best companies prepare for smooth succession; more importantly, it tells all of us to take succession planning far more seriously. Doing so assures the continuity of organizations and the ideas that propel them. Mentoring people, nurturing them, carefully planning for the time when you yourself will move on to another stage in your life is doing nothing more than sustaining the legacy of your life's work.

In addition to this ongoing, long-term agenda, companies are increasingly recognizing the importance of planning for the unexpected. A CEO who is healthy and vital one day may become gravely ill or die the next. Just as suddenly, CEOs now often make surprise moves to other companies. Hence, more and more boards are insisting on "drop-in" candidates—who may or may not be permanent successors—ready to step in as a replacement CEO on a moment's notice.

The critical importance of succession planning is understood by too few people. The truth is, many chief executives view succession as a threat to their own status or livelihood and spend very little time wondering who their successors will be. That's understandable: It's human nature to think that, if you're the top dog, no one else can do your job. Yet, nine years before his expected retirement as chief executive of General Electric Company, Jack Welch was already saying that choosing his successor was "the most important decision I'll make. It occupies a considerable amount of thought almost every day."

And well it should. Much of today's spotlight on CEO succession comes in the wake of a series of bloody dustups that have filled the business pages of late. For far too many companies, succession at the top has become a messy melodrama, the result of poor preparation, out-of-control egos, and bad choices. When succession becomes a struggle and a problem, it not only threatens the current and future success of an organization, it also threatens the legacy of those who worked so hard to create and build something that is enduring.

Not surprisingly, then, much attention has been paid in recent years to how succession is planned and executed. Major changes have occurred in the field, many of them explored in this book. The changes are partly due to pressure from institutional shareholders and partly to the acknowledged importance of having the brightest, most creative people on board. The massive downsizings of the 1980s and 1990s that have weakened the bench strength of many companies have also played a role. They've made companies far more willing than before to go outside their ranks for a new CEO. Back in the late 1960s, only 9 percent of new leaders came from outside. Now, nearly a third of the CEOs at America's top one thousand public corporations are outsiders—and that number is likely to grow.

But the biggest change may simply be the influence directors now wield in the process. Choosing a successor was once the near-exclusive province of the outgoing boss, who would present his pick to a generally compliant board. Now, outside directors at companies ranging from Campbell Soup to Merck and General Motors are taking a bigger hand in selecting the new boss. In the past, the onus to groom a successor was largely placed on the incumbent CEO. Today the onus for developing and finding a successor has moved to the board of directors.

With the direct involvement of the chief executive, every board must work toward the inevitable transition that will lead to new leadership. A goal of every executive and every manager is to cultivate talent. A goal of every CEO is to expose and test that talent before a board of directors and the outside world. If board members find the CEO is unwilling to face this part of his job, they need to forcefully remind the boss that it is within his best interests to worry not only about the company's strategy and focus but also about its leadership.

In the landmark study on what accounted for the long-term success of the truly visionary corporations, James C. Collins and Jerry I. Pooras correctly noted in *Built to Last* that the best companies "promote from within to preserve the core." They spend the money, the time, and the energy to develop, promote, and select talent from inside the company to a greater degree than their less successful rivals. Indeed, Collins and Pooras found that across seventeen hundred years of combined history in their eighteen visionary companies, there were only four individual cases of an outsider coming directly into the role of chief executive.

How to explain, then, the willingness of major companies to look outside their own ranks for a new CEO? While many organizations still devote significant effort to grooming up-and-coming executives, a decade or more of white-collar layoffs has drained a lot of talent from the pool. It has also cut layers of management where high-potential executives once gained additional seasoning.

Some observers now think that rapid changes in business and a more mobile job market have made much of the talk about management development meaningless for the run-of-the-mill company. "Unless you're GE or somebody like that, it may no longer make economic sense to make major investments in development and training," says Robery Felton, a McKinsey & Co. partner. "Companies should think twice about spending a lot of time and money on someone who may walk out of the door anyway. A healthier attitude today may be to consider the world as your bench."

That's still, of course, an unusual view, one that I do not share. But it is a view that is prompted in part by the inability of organizations that have spent more money and time on management development than any others—IBM and AT&T—to cultivate internal CEOs. "They prepared a wonderful group of executives for yesterday's business," believes Edward E. Lawler, director of the Center for Effective Organizations at the University of Southern California. "By being so good at narrowing the gene pool, they replicated people who would have been good business leaders in the past but not the future."

Lawler's observation, however, should not lead organizations to forgo efforts to develop and nurture inside talent. Neither should it be a call to recruit solely from the outside. Instead, it should underline the need for chief executives and boards to pay close attention to the process of management development and succession. CEOs and directors must envision what their organizations will need not now but in the future. This is the kind of crystal ball gazing, the kind of forward-looking rumination, that led GE chairman Reginald Jones in 1981 to pick the most unlikely of successors, an organizational radical and change agent who became one of this century's greatest leaders. There is a Jack Welch in nearly every organization, waiting to be encouraged, nourished, and cultivated, waiting to rise to the top. It's the job of the CEO and the board to make sure he or she surfaces.

Years ago, a friend and colleague at *Business Week* magazine confided that he had three goals in life: to have a son, to plant a tree, and to write a book. In his search for purpose and immortality, he might just as well have added a fourth goal: to mentor a person who might well carry on the business and purpose of his life. That, my friends, is the true nature of succession. It is the best motivation for why we should so carefully plan for the future.

We would like to dedicate this book to our clients, without whom this book would not have been possible. They willingly and enthusiastically shared their own experiences, providing the company perspectives we believed were essential. These lessons, combined with our own views, should encourage directors and CEOs to devote to succession planning—one of the most important business issues today—the time and attention it deserves. We would also like to express our warmest appreciation to Judith Roland, a first-class writer, who helped us craft thousands of pages of research into a coherent, useful, and, we hope, interesting book.

Dennis Carey
Dayton Ogden

The reader should bear in mind that profiles of specific individuals and companies in this book should be viewed as snapshots in time. We worked as meticulously as possible, prepublication, to ensure that all company names and individuals' titles were as up-to-date as possible. But, particularly in a dynamic business environment, there are the inevitable changes in the status and names of companies, as well as the status and titles of the executives who work for them. Any such changes, we believe, are relatively minor and should not detract from the mission of this book: to illuminate best practices in CEO succession planning.

1

Introduction

In late March of 1996, Richard Swift, CEO of Foster Wheeler Corporation, a $4.5 billion New Jersey-based engineering and construction giant, was invited by then secretary of commerce Ron Brown to participate in a U.S. trade mission to Bosnia. Because of other demands on his time, Swift had to decline. But Robert A. Whittaker, vice president of Foster Wheeler's Energy Equipment Group and president of Foster Wheeler Energy International, believed it was important for the company to be represented and volunteered to participate. As the world now knows, the plane carrying Brown, Whittaker, and eleven other corporate executives crashed in the Bosnian mountains, killing all of them.

The loss of a key executive—a group head and direct report to the CEO—did not leave a gaping hole in the organization, though it was deeply felt by those in the company, because Foster Wheeler's board had planned ahead. While no one could have predicted the air crash tragedy, the company was, in a practical sense, prepared for it. Long before the Bosnia trip, Foster Wheeler's board of directors had put in place a comprehensive succession plan for its top executives, one designed precisely to deal with unanticipated events. From the board's perspective, avoiding any long-term disruption in its leadership ranks was a critical part of corporate governance.

Unfortunately many other companies, including those that lost senior officers in the Bosnia airplane crash, weren't nearly as prescient. Among those caught unprepared were ABB, Inc., a subsidiary of the $31 billion Swiss company ABB Asea Brown Boveri Ltd., whose president and CEO, Robert Donovan, died in the crash. Immediately following the crash, a spokeswoman for the company was quoted in the *Wall Street Journal* as saying that the company had prepared only for an interim appointment. Similarly, the spokesman for the Bechtel Group, which lost P. Stuart Tholan, senior vice president and president, Bechtel Europe, Middle East, and Southwest Asia, stated that he had "no idea" who would succeed Tholan, adding, "We do have detailed succession planning," without elaborating further.

The Message Hits Home

The deaths of a dozen U.S. executives from prominent companies killed in the Bosnia plane crash in 1996 underscored the critical importance of succession planning as never before. Given the magnitude of the loss, it would have been impossible for other companies not to identify with it. How easy it would be for anyone to suffer a similar fate to those on the Bosnia mission—whether in a plane crash, automobile accident, or as a result of an illness. Suddenly the subject of succession was front and center, but once the story receded from the headlines, most companies got back to more pressing business concerns.

Because identifying leaders is the heart of our business, succession has always been a major concern of ours, but an experience several years ago drove home, in a very personal way, just how crucial a process it should be for all companies. In early spring 1996 we met with Jerry Junkins, then CEO of Texas Instruments, in his office in Dallas to discuss corporate governance issues.

When we broached the subject of succession planning, and who would replace him in the event of a crisis, Junkins responded confidently: "I'm as lean and healthy as a horse." The company, he told us, had a succession plan in place to coincide with his planned retirement. But that was not scheduled for another two to three years, and there was no apparent reason to speed the process up. A few months later, Junkins died of a massive heart attack in the backseat of his car while visiting a customer in Europe. Texas Instruments—left without an immediate successor—was thrown into turmoil.

In our experience, stories such as these are far from unique. In fact, there have been a rather rapidly increasing number of succession disasters in recent years that should serve as cautionary tales for directors, reminding them to act before it is too late. Whether precipitated by sudden tragedy, CEO performance issues, a CEO simply picking up and going elsewhere, or retiring, there is no question that succession has become a front-burner issue for directors. Yet in spite of the growing emphasis on succession planning, there is virtually nothing written on the topic from a practical point of view, leaving individual companies to fend for themselves and more or less reinvent the wheel each time they begin the process.

Since we recruit both CEOs and directors for client companies, unlike even the best-informed observer, we are privy to all that goes on, both in public and behind the scenes. And because we have worked for years with many leading companies in a variety of industries, we've seen a wide range of scenarios played out, giving us a good sense of what does and does not work. Given the expanded focus by directors on succession planning—combined with the fact that there is virtually nothing in the business literature to guide them in the process—we wondered: Might there be a way to quantify "best practices" in succession planning? Could we fill the void by combining our collective experience working with clients on succession-related matters with an up-close look at selected companies known for having a well-developed succession process?

With this agenda in mind, we began our research for this book on succession planning in August 1996. Less than a year later, we had completed interviews with CEOs and top human resources executives at a dozen companies: Metropolitan Life, Caterpillar, Hewlett-Packard, Mobil, Continental Grain, SmithKline Beecham, Delta, Mellon Bank, Bestfoods, Foster Wheeler, Hercules, and GTE. The companies we selected are generally recognized as leaders in their fields, represent a fairly representative cross section of American industry, and have a systematic succession planning process in place. In particular, we sought companies that were known to us for achieving success in at least one succession-related practice—for example, significant board involvement, a strong leadership development focus, planning well in advance for a variety of eventualities. We supplemented these initial interviews by tapping literally scores of CEOs and directors for specific input on a variety of issues as we developed each chapter.

What Works?

We asked those we interviewed to lead us through their succession process and posed a number of specific questions geared to illuminate key elements such as roles and responsibilities, communication, and timing. Long before we completed the interviews, a clear picture began to emerge regarding systematic steps and best practices being undertaken by these leading companies (these will be discussed in detail in the chapters that follow):

- *One lesson that has emerged from our research and observations is that strong boards that are not afraid to challenge and prod the CEO when necessary will also take a major role in crafting and maintaining momentum for a well-thought-out succession planning processes.* At any successful company, of course, the board and CEO must work together effectively as a team, but as representatives of the shareholders and overseers of management, it is essential that boards play more than a reactive role in the succession process and keep the CEO on track. As with estate planning, there is a natural tendency for people to avoid planning for their own obsolescence. Because planning for continuity of leadership is so critical to the long-term health of an organization, it is therefore the board's responsibility to hold the CEO's feet to the fire on succession issues.

- *Succession planning should not be viewed as a phenomenon that occurs only at the very top of an organization.* Limiting the objective of succession planning merely to designating a replacement from among the CEO's direct reports is a little like a ship's captain seeing only the tip of the iceberg. An integral part of any succession plan is an organizational development process that continually emphasizes identifying high-potential executives and provides them with opportunities to grow and develop. Companies that are successful in doing this do not have to worry about the leadership well running dry, as they are constantly renewing the source.

- *The board has to be kept up to date on high-potential employees at all levels. And, at regular intervals, the board must challenge and prod the CEO about the development process, particularly when it comes to grooming potential CEO successors.* Directors will want to assess the progress of potential successors and be kept informed of what the company is doing to round out their skills and experience.

- *Even companies with strong cultures that have been highly successful in leadership development are increasingly calibrating internal candidates for CEO against comparable outside leaders.* Some companies do this on a periodic basis, and we see this even in cases where the choice for CEO will almost certainly be an insider. Why? Because it's a way of seeing how these candidates stack up against those in comparable positions in the industry and ensuring that the best possible leader is tapped from the broadest possible universe.

- *Directors should consider structuring specific financial incentives to better assure success in succession planning.* According to what we have observed, boards are increasingly requiring CEOs to report regularly on succession-planning activities with various contingency plans and are formally linking diligence in this area to the CEO's bonus opportunity. Moreover, boards are aggressively "handcuffing" next-generation CEOs, making it less likely that companies will lose valuable resources they may have spent years developing and investing in. There is also a growing realization that directors themselves will take succession more seriously when their thinking is better aligned with shareholders and their own economic interests are at stake. Thus directors are increasingly being paid in stock, and an increasing number of companies are requiring directors to make a personal investment in the company.

- *There are practices that boards should be wary of because of their potential to undermine the succession process.* For example, we think boards should carefully assess all alternatives before appointing one of their own outside directors as CEO. Having directors on a board who are aspiring CEOs can create unnecessary conflict and politicize the process, and we believe that appointing directors as CEO should be considered a practice of last resort. Mergers and acquisitions can also disrupt the succession process. CEO designates can be dislodged from their next-in-line position when a top executive from the merger partner becomes a serious contender for the CEO spot, as occurred with the Bell Atlantic/Nynex and ABC/Disney mergers. Though there is some evidence to suggest that companies may look to mergers and acquisitions as way of addressing succession issues; clearly, in this regard, these transactions may create as many problems as they solve.

Power Shift to Boards

We urge boards to actively begin to manage the succession process, not only because of all that is at stake when the process goes awry—to a great extent this has always been the case—but also because for the first time in the history of American corporate governance, boards have sufficient clout and independence to undertake this task.

There has been nothing short of a revolution in the structure and practices of corporate boards over the past dozen or so years, based on our experience as well as data we collect annually on corporate boards. This change is largely a result of the rapidly growing presence and influence of independent outside directors overseeing the corporate governance process on behalf of shareholders. According to the data from Spencer Stuart's Board Index, an annual proxy analysis of the largest U.S. companies and leaders in corporate governance, ten years ago the ratio of inside directors to outside directors was 2.5:1, while currently the ratio is 3.5:1—a seismic shift in a little over ten years.

What significance does all this hold for the CEO succession planning process? It stands to reason that outside directors—especially those observed at close range by shareholder groups and the media—will be less inclined to fall into lockstep with the CEO and will take their fiduciary responsibilities more to heart. As the ratio around the boardroom table has shifted to a preponderance of outsiders, the balance of power has shifted as well. One measure of this shift is the number of CEOs who have been toppled in recent years—including once-revered CEOs such as James Robinson at American Express, John Akers at IBM, Kay Whitmore at Kodak, and Robert Stempel at General Motors—by boards that have apparently been dissatisfied with the CEO's performance. Directors, ever conscious of their fiduciary responsibilities, are increasingly identifying with the interests of shareholders and demonstrating an unprecedented tendency to get rid of the CEO when they perceive strategic failure or faltering stock performance.

CEOs leave companies voluntarily, too. There is undoubtedly more movement of CEOs and other top managers from one company to another, even across industries, than in the past. Factor in the perennial uncertainty of life in general; the CEO still, like all of us, may fall victim to accident or illness. With the plethora of high-profile reminders about CEO mortality at companies such as Coca-Cola, Tenneco, Texas Instruments, and Frontier, it is easy to understand why companies face the increased likelihood of being left leaderless, with fewer guarantees that a candidate one level down in the organization will be available to fill the hole.

When a public company is left with a void in leadership, for whatever reason, the ripple effects are widely felt both within and outside the organization. Internally, a company is likely to suffer a crisis of morale, confidence, and productivity among employees and, similarly, stockholders may panic when a company is left rudderless and worry about the safety and future of their investment.

Given the current climate of CEO movement, the number and severity of the problems companies may face when they lose a CEO, and the much-monitored fiduciary duties of directors, it is not surprising that companies are paying a good deal more attention to CEO succession planning and the underlying leadership development process. Interestingly, this planning process differs significantly from that of the past in many important respects: in the way it is conceived, carried out, and, most especially, in who is viewed as being in control of the process.

A Board-Managed Process

In the past, the succession process was a much more informal one and considered very much in the domain of the CEO. CEOs not only determined the timing, but also who would succeed them and how much preparation the successor would get to assume the role. The outcome and ultimate success of the process depended almost exclusively on the judgment, skills, motivation, and attitude of the individual CEO.

The influx of outside directors on most public company boards and the net loss of insiders means boards are no longer as willing to leave such a crucial task as succession planning within the control of the CEO. With their fiduciary duties on behalf of shareholders repeatedly impressed on them, outside directors are coming to realize that, in fact, they have no more vital or fundamental a responsibility than to ensure the continuity of effective leadership, the lifeblood of any organization.

The lessons of past corporate history—and human behavior throughout the ages—and the many less-than-successful succession stories have served as warnings for boards charged with protecting the investments of shareholders. On examination, succession planning turns out to be a highly complex process, where CEOs may experience a number of conflicting emotions and motivations. It seems only logical, therefore, that while the CEO should develop succession alternatives, the board must manage the ultimate decision-making process for optimal results.

For one thing, it is human nature to avoid dealing with those things that entail planning for one's own demise. How else does one explain the fact that most people, even highly successful ones with significant assets, procrastinate when it comes to drawing up wills and appointing guardians for their children? Similarly, when it comes to succession planning, rather than confront their own mortality and plan for death, accident, or even normal retirement, the vast majority of CEOs have done an inadequate job. The dozens of companies that have been left in the lurch and suffered as the result of the sudden death or departure of a CEO who did not plan for his or her own replacement serve as testament to this.

Even in the grip of a terminal illness, when they are aware that the end is near, some CEOs find it impossible to face the inevitable and name a successor. Following the death of Coca-Cola CEO Roberto C. Goizueta in October 1997, the *Wall Street Journal* ran a story titled, "To Tell, or Not to Tell, When the CEO Is Sick." According to the article, when Time Warner chairman and co-CEO Steven Ross was battling prostate cancer in the year preceding his death in late 1992, "the media giant continued to insist Mr. Ross was still running the show during much of that time. Insiders 'didn't want to hurt Steve' by revealing that 'he was working from home in great pain' and only a few hours a day, one Ross acquaintance recollects. Mr. Ross also worried that wider knowledge of his weakened state might crimp his control of succession. Prior to his death late at night in his New York hospital room, that was 'all he would talk about: Who should be his successor?' his friend continued."

When CEOs do plan for their own succession, results are often problematic. It is not uncommon for CEOs to keep succession plans close to the vest, keeping them secret even from directors. Results of such "planning" are frequently haphazard and hard to predict: A successor may eventually be announced; an indeterminate timetable may be established; a "horse race" may be set up among leading contenders for the CEO spot, greatly increasing the chances that major players may defect when a winner is selected and the succession plan is put into effect.

Why is it that all does not often go well when the CEO holds the succession reins? Perhaps it is because, frequently, high-powered executives do not relinquish power voluntarily or know when it is time to move on. Wittingly or unwittingly, CEOs can disrupt the succession process in a number of ways: They may not select the most capable successor or may remain too involved—during the transition period or after, especially if the outgoing CEO remains on the board—and may even sabotage the efforts of the new CEO.

Although CEOs generally have far greater familiarity with top managers and their abilities than anyone else on the board, and the CEO's constant input is essential to the outcome of the process, it is becoming evident that CEOs should not be calling all the shots, assigning succession-related tasks, and establishing the timetable for the change.

We urge CEOs and boards to break from the hasty, superficial, and intuitive approach to succession and to substitute instead a systematic, predictable, and transparent process throughout their entire management organization.

Currents and Undercurrents

Consider the following trends:

- the emergence of the predominance and power of outside directors on corporate boards;
- constant cries from the media and shareholder activists for these directors to fulfill their fiduciary duties and provide a stronger counterbalance to the CEO;
- the increasingly high turnover and generally short tenure of CEOs of major public companies (according to Spencer Stuart data, the average tenure as CEO at *Fortune* 100 companies is seven years);
- the growing realization that ensuring continuity of leadership is a board's most important responsibility.

Given these concomitant developments, it is not difficult to understand why more and more boards are taking control and establishing the agenda for the succession process. There is simply too much at stake, too great a risk of chaos and the consequent negative effects—internally and externally—when a company has, for whatever reason, lost a CEO and cannot promptly announce to the world, including the investment community, that a capable successor is prepared to take over. We don't believe we're being melodramatic when we insist that a company's very survival may depend upon a well-thought-out and carefully executed succession plan.

But how are companies to know what constitutes best practices for this critical activity? Trial and error doesn't seem a very practical or sensible approach with so much at stake and the repercussions from failure so potentially disastrous. After having the opportunity to observe, up close, what some leading companies are doing in the area of succession planning, we thought it would be instructive to assemble some best practices from companies that have done it well so that others could learn from what has worked for these leaders.

Learning from Others

The lessons we learned from the best practices of these leaders form the structure of this book. After chapter 1, each succeeding chapter describes an important element in succession planning that has been used by companies that have successfully carried out the succession process. They also include examples of companies whose successions failed to work as planned. Companies that are able to put in place all of the lessons we learned should be able to confront the succession process with confidence.

In chapter 2, "Covering All the Bases," we explore the range of scenarios companies should be planning for, including normal retirement, incapacitation, or death of the CEO. Those companies that have planned only for the CEO's normal retirement have not done a thorough job and could be placing the investments of shareholders at risk. Boards and CEOs may want to consider a sort of "corporate-twenty-fifth amendment" that, much as in the case of temporary illness or a catastrophe with the president, kicks a coping strategy into action.

In chapter 3, "Putting a Process in Place," we get into the actual nuts and bolts of succession planning and how a board can establish and sustain a reliable succession agenda and timetable with the CEO to ensure that succession-related responsibilities are defined, assigned, and discharged on an ongoing basis.

In chapter 4, "Looking Deep Within the Organization," we explore how companies can implement a true self-renewing succession culture that will enable them to continually develop leaders throughout their organization. Companies that are able to institutionalize a leadership development process that penetrates the layers of management don't have to worry about gaps in leadership, at the top or at any other layer, as they are continually developing new leaders to take their place.

Chapter 5, "Striking the Right Balance Between the Board and the CEO," examines a process that is tricky to get just right but that is crucial to the success of the entire succession process. It needs to be "cordial, but not too cozy," as one of the human resources executives we interviewed so aptly put it. We discuss the sort of healthy dialogue that should be taking place between the board and the CEO and how the board can help the CEO to stay on track regarding succession.

As we detail in chapter 6, "The Delicate Matter of the 'Number Two'," the board needs to have plenty of exposure to those next in line to the CEO before they are faced with decisions about actual successors. In this chapter we examine how boards can best form a multidimensional view of next-generation CEOs so that when a succession decision must be made, boards can make informed selections.

In chapter 7, "Financial Tools That Promote Succession Planning," we present a range of financial tools companies can use with each of the parties in the succession planning process—CEOs, successors, and directors—to ensure that each performs to the best of his or her ability and maximizes the chances of a successful outcome.

As we discuss in chapter 8, "Global Intelligence®: A Window on the World," even those companies that have established a reliable succession process find there is great value and comfort in calibrating internal candidates for CEO and other top posts with comparable outside leaders. Here we explore the hows and the whys of this increasingly common check companies are using to, as one of the CEOs we interviewed said, "keep ourselves honest."

Practices that we refer to in chapter 9, "Flashing Yellow Light: Potential Problems Ahead," may be undertaken by companies during the succession planning process but are not necessarily recommended. Companies that appoint outside directors as CEOs or have directors serve as mentors to potential successors, for example, should be aware of the pitfalls as well as the pluses that may be inherent in these approaches to succession. In addition, we address the increasing volume of corporate mergers and acquisitions and the peculiar issues they raise in addressing succession issues.

In chapter 10, "Conclusion: Core Principles Yield Best Practices," we give some final guidelines for boards that recognize the urgency of greater director involvement in the succession planning process and are ready to take constructive action. We hope we have equipped boards and CEOs with the knowledge and the tools they need to make an impact in this crucial area.

We believe that a growing number of boards are increasingly cognizant of their responsibility regarding the succession planning process and understand the need to establish a systematic process. For these enlightened and committed boards, this book can serve as a guide to shaping specific strategy based on what has worked in other companies and what has not. For boards that may be all too ready to relinquish responsibility for succession planning, we fervently hope that this book will serve as a wake-up call.

2

Covering All the Bases

"I thought I'd have six months to a year to learn the basics, but after only six weeks, God took him."

—Joseph Clayton, former CEO of Frontier Corporation, referring to his predecessor, Ronald Bittner, who died of a brain tumor.

There was evidently a great deal of shock and sadness at Coca-Cola when CEO Roberto C. Goizueta—who had built a near fifty-year career at the company—died soon after being diagnosed with "treatable" lung cancer. But his death did nothing to disrupt the carefully orchestrated succession process, and an able and well-prepared successor was immediately available. There was no secrecy, no particular fanfare in connection with announcing the successor; it was merely the next and final logical step in the self-renewing management development process Goizueta himself had helped to implement.

An article that appeared in *Business Week* soon after Goizueta's death on October 18, 1997, observed: "To Goizueta, succession was the logical culmination of a program he designed to develop and promote talented people. He saw the decision to delegate authority as one of his three main tasks, along with his stewardship of corporate finance and his managing of Coke's reputation. And he saw designating a successor as the ultimate act of delegation.

"Goizueta first saw Ivester [M. Douglas Ivester, his successor as CEO] as a comer in 1983 when the former accountant squeezed millions in cash flow out of movie payments not due Coke for years. During the 1980s he toughened him with challenging assignments. Meanwhile, Goizueta developed more than a dozen talented executives under Ivester.

"The lessons of Ivester's appointment will live on at Coke. 'It's bigger than just having a succession plan,' says board member Susan B. King. 'For years, Coke has been identifying, maintaining, and developing the best young talent. It's not something that happens overnight.'"

At Coke, succession was something far bigger than the CEO. Many companies, however, maintain a rigidly narrow definition of the succession process—that is, planning for the routine retirement of the CEO when his or her term has been completed. Once they have tackled this aspect of succession, they feel that they have done their work and can rest easy. This scenario is, of course, an important one to plan for, but equally important are the more immediate possibilities—the ones that can really catch companies by surprise and can have disastrous consequences. Indeed, there are a range of possibilities when it comes to succession, and while companies cannot plan for every imaginable eventuality, there are several typical scenarios for which companies can prepare and have a game plan ready to put into action if and when necessary. This chapter is devoted to a discussion of this sort of contingency planning.

The concept of succession planning has evolved in recent years. Once viewed as a "process" that existed only in the mind of the CEO and was defined as the designation of a successor if and when the CEO deemed necessary, succession planning today is viewed as a far more complex process, with many levels and layers. The discretionary duties and timetables of CEOs and directors have given way to much more defined and structured corporate governance responsibilities. High expectations and vigilance from shareholders and the media have increased pressure on boards to ensure that all the bases are covered and that no matter what the circumstances facing a company, an effective leader will be ready to step in and take over, on a moment's notice if necessary.

What does "having all the bases covered" mean these days? It means that, working together, the CEO and the board should have a contingency plan and successors ready to implement in response to all of the most common succession scenarios that may confront a company, including:

- incapacitating illness or sudden demise of the CEO;

- replacing an underperforming CEO;

- surprise departure of the CEO;

- normal retirement.

In the balance of this chapter we examine these contingencies, and describe some of the ways in which companies have anticipated and planned for them effectively—as well as cases where they have failed to plan for them—and the consequences that followed.

Frontier: Assume the Worst

In August 1997 Joseph Clayton became CEO of Frontier, a local, long-distance, and wireless telecommunications company. He held the position until September 1999 when Frontier was acquired by Global Crossing, Ltd., of which Clayton is now vice chairman. When speaking with him about succession planning, one senses the relief of someone who has just made a narrow escape. When Clayton was brought on board in June 1997 as president/COO, there had been no next-in-command to the CEO since May 1996, when William H. Oberlin resigned to become CEO of MIDCOM Communications, Inc.

Frontier had been through a bit of a rocky year internally to that point. Ronald Bittner, CEO at the time, had undergone emergency surgery on New Year's Eve for a brain tumor. Bittner's condition came as a surprise to everyone in the company, and while it was obviously very serious, he was, according to Clayton, "back in the saddle within thirty days," and the official word from the company expressed optimism for a complete recovery.

The unofficial word was not nearly so hopeful. We vividly recall a meeting soon after Bittner's surgery, at a time when both he and the board were displaying great confidence publicly about his continued leadership of the company. The sentiments that Bittner expressed in private, however, were a very different story. He made this clear to us in discussing the leadership prospects of the company president, only forty-one at the time and not yet ready to take over the duties of CEO.

"He'd be great four or five years from now, but I'm going to die," Bittner said in a surprisingly matter-of-fact manner. "I need someone now."

Frontier had not ignored the need to plan for succession. Before Bittner had even become aware of his illness we had been brought in to do a search for a president who would ultimately become CEO as part of a planned retirement scenario. What the company had not addressed was the importance of contingency planning: planning for a variety of possible scenarios and different time frames. Frontier's board and CEO had anticipated and planned for the expected long-term challenge but not for the potential ambush.

Now in crisis mode, the board was split between biding its time with the inside candidate and quickly looking for an immediate successor to fill Bittner's shoes. Dan Gill, chairman of the board's search committee, was the driving force on the board for going for a strong immediate candidate. Coincidentally, Gill had recently been through the same illness with a close relative, who had lasted less than a year, so he knew firsthand how quickly Bittner's fortunes and health could change, though the surgery had apparently gone well. "I think we'd be well advised to assume the worst," Gill told us before we began the search.

There was much discussion among board members on how best to proceed, and there was a great deal of concern that moving too rapidly would hurt Ron and exacerbate his already serious condition. In the end, the board decided with Ron that it would be in the best interest of the company and its shareholders to embark on a search for a number two who would be guaranteed the CEO position within twelve months.

Our search, therefore, was not for the typical number two executive who would remain in that position for a given period of time until a retirement or other longer-term scenario played out. We would be looking for a CEO who would temporarily function as the number two but who would be guaranteed the actual CEO title in very short order. These terms were clearly spelled out with serious candidates during the course of our search, with the company agreeing to adhere to the time frame and certain economic assurances to help us attract a truly outstanding successor. Understandably, it is extremely difficult to attract current CEOs to what is perceived as a number two spot, but given circumstances such as those at Frontier and the guarantees of the board, we were able to attract CEOs who might otherwise be scared off by the prospect of an open-ended heir apparent situation.

Despite failing health, particularly toward the end of the search process, Bittner played a significant role in assisting our firm and the board to evaluate finalists for the position and spent a great deal of time with Clayton, the successful candidate, helping him to understand all of the major challenges confronting the business.

Having come this close to being left without a CEO, you can bet that Clayton and his board thought long and hard, and made changes accordingly, so that they could avoid such a close call in the future.

"One of the things that could really have created confusion at Frontier was the fact that there was no president/COO—if there is no clear successor, you foster too much competition among department heads. Having a president/COO would have made succession smoother," says Clayton, qualifying his position as he presents a clearer picture of the precise set of circumstances that Frontier faced. "Of course, that's when things are going hunky-dory. When you're dealing with internal candidates from a regulated environment, they might not be prepared for the free-market swing," such as that Frontier was experiencing at the time of the transition from one CEO to another.

"The skill base is different. I come from the consumer electronics business—the most competitive business there is today. I wasn't polluted by the past, and while I didn't have a lot of telecommunications experience, I did have turnaround experience in a formerly regulated business. The board had to weigh the issue of an insider versus an outsider as CEO, and they decided they needed to recruit someone who could bring about a dramatic change in the direction of the business and force a cultural shift within the company." An important element for the board to consider, of course, was that there was not a natural successor within the organization.

In his first few months as CEO, Clayton focused on what he viewed as "the basics": building his team, putting a plan in place, and divesting the company of nonstrategic assets. But he and the board were also mindful of the need to strengthen their top-management bench so that whenever a successor would be needed—whether according to a longer-range plan or on a moment's notice, as was the case with Clayton—Frontier would be ready. To help develop leadership in an environment where senior managers had traditionally spent a great deal of time competing with one another, Clayton made significant promotions at the second and third levels of management.

It was fortunate that Frontier's board acted as quickly as it did. Frontier might easily have been left without a clear successor, compounding the tragedy of Bittner's death with confusion, lack of direction, and possibly worse for the company and its shareholders.

The Right to Know: When Should Shareholders Be Told of a CEO's Illness?

Three years before Ronald Bittner died of a brain tumor, Tenneco, Inc., CEO Michael Walsh suffered the same fate. A *Wall Street Journal* article that appeared immediately following the death of Coca-Cola's CEO, Roberto Goizueta, in October 1997 contrasted the way in which Frontier's and Tenneco's CEOs and boards dealt with the same tragic crisis with their CEO's health.

Unlike Bittner, Walsh chose the full-disclosure route when he got the news of his brain tumor, including issuing an immediate press release, holding a news conference, and releasing the corporate doctor's letter to directors outlining the course of treatment. According to the *Journal,* "Walsh also prepared a videotape for the conglomerate's nearly 80,000 employees worldwide. The tape 'quieted the rumor mills that might otherwise have been springing up,' remembers Mark Andrews, a Tenneco board member.

"But the CEO's candor was emotionally wrenching for some staffers. During the twenty-two-minute tape, Mr. Walsh's hoarse voice occasionally cracked with emotion when he described the anxiety of waiting for a confirmed diagnosis. Managers in Germany, France, Britain, and parts of Southeast Asia refused to show the tape because Mr. Walsh was so openly vulnerable and frank."

When the same article references the situation at Frontier, it poses the question of why the company did not disclose Bittner's true condition until just before he died. "'Nobody was prepared to say that we thought he would die,' recalls Leo Thomas, a Frontier director and retired Eastman Kodak executive vice president."

Upon consideration of the cases of Frontier and Tenneco, we have two companies faced with a similar set of circumstances—both high-profile, large public companies with CEOs fighting the same life-threatening illness—who take very different tacks in disclosing the illness. All this begs these questions: Is there a "right" way to handle these situations? What are the variables companies need to consider?

We'd like to state, unequivocally and loudly and clearly upfront, that as the legal representatives of the shareholders, the board must be aware of any health condition that may adversely affect the CEO's ability to competently execute his or her responsibilities. Whether or when any such health condition needs to made public, including to shareholders, is a different matter. Since being able to plan for continuity of the CEO's responsibilities is a critical element of the board's fiduciary duties, the CEO must immediately notify the board committee charged with responsibility for succession if he or she becomes aware of a life-threatening illness.

Obviously, a serious health threat to the CEO presents not only a difficult and potentially precarious situation for the company but also for the CEO personally. As we see it, there is little to be gained from broadcasting the CEO's health concerns to constituencies outside the boardroom, at least initially. Directors need to be mindful of protecting the CEO's right to privacy, when appropriate, as long as they are providing for the company's ongoing leadership needs.

There is also a lot to be said for protecting shareholders from themselves. Broadcasting news of a health-threatening illness to shareholders could well create a panic that could prove disastrous for the company, so such a move is unnecessary—indeed, unwise—unless and until the CEO is incapacitated.

According to Nell Minow, a principal of LENS, well-known and vocal activist money managers, a responsibility of the board, such as managing the succession of a terminally ill CEO, becomes the responsibility of shareholders only when things reach a crisis point because the board refuses to address the issue. "It's the responsibility of shareholders," she says, to make sure the board does its job, not to do the board's job for them."

As a result of LENS's experience and observation of various companies, Minow says that her partner, Bob Monk, has concluded that businesses go through the same stages as those defined by Elisabeth Kübler-Ross in her landmark book *Death and Dying*, the first stage being denial of one's own mortality. At one company she is familiar with, directors got into a screaming fight with the CEO when they tried to plan with him how succession would be handled should he die suddenly. "The CEO kept insisting that he wasn't going to die," Minow related. Following this incident, directors staged what is commonly referred to in popular psychology as an "intervention." As a group, they confronted the CEO and let him know that he was hurting the company. Fortunately, the confrontation produced positive results, and directors were able to get the CEO's cooperation on developing a succession process.

Texas Instruments: Buying Time

Like Frontier, Texas Instruments lost a CEO under tragic circumstances. Unlike Frontier, it had a clear successor in mind, though the board determined that that successor was not immediately ready to take over all of former CEO Jerry Junkins' combined duties of chairman and CEO. An exceedingly strong internal culture necessitated remaining with an internal solution rather than considering an outsider who would instantly be able to step into Junkins' complete role. Under these circumstances, which though not common are far from unique, how does a company hold on to a chosen successor who needs a bit more experience before assuming both the CEO and chairman roles?

This was an important question TI's board had to consider when Junkins died suddenly of a heart attack in May 1996. The heir apparent whom he had assured us would be ready in two to three years was needed now, and the board had to determine how best to deal with the void. Not only did directors have to deal with the shock of losing the longtime chairman, CEO, and president, they also had to immediately respond to his death with a plan detailing who would now continue to carry out his responsibilities.

The internal successor they had in mind, Thomas Engibous, brought significant qualifications and tremendous promise. At the time of Junkins' death, Engibous was executive vice president and president of TI's Semiconductor Group, the company's largest business, making him an appealing candidate for outside job offers.

The board faced the issue squarely, engaging in an extensive debate about how to ensure effective corporate leadership until Engibous was ready, while at the same time dealing with him openly and fairly to keep him from succumbing to the overtures that would likely come his way.

The board recognized the obvious problem: The company had counted on time to groom its strongest candidate for CEO. Realizing that they had run out of time, they were able to buy some with the solution they crafted. For the brief period directors reckoned they would need coverage for governance duties, directors opted for an inside solution to temporarily fill the gap, rather than bringing in an outside solution that might have sent a very different message to Engibous. The board called on member John Adams, a well-respected retired executive with a reputation as a leader, to serve as interim chairman, with Engibous as president and CEO until he was fully prepared to assume both roles.

This move by the board proved to be an excellent temporary solution to a temporary problem. Fortunately for TI, Adams, along with vice chairmen William Mitchell and William "Pat" Weber (who oversaw daily operations in the immediate aftermath of Junkins' death), were well known to analysts, reassuring Wall Street about the company's immediate future. All went according to plan. In February 1998 Engibous took over the combined role of chairman, president, and CEO, and in April of the same year, Weber retired. TI was indeed lucky to have an internal successor as well as a director capable of stepping into the chairman's role to ensure a smooth transition.

Becton, Dickinson: The Brave New World of CEO Mobility

On June 6, 1994, the *Wall Street Journal* reported, with surprise, that "Merck & Co. directors had reached outside the company and unexpectedly picked Raymond V. Gilmartin of Becton, Dickinson and Co. (BD) as its next chairman and CEO," a position he was to fill only a few days hence. "In selecting Mr. Gilmartin as the first outsider to lead the company," the *Journal* announcement continued, "the Merck board had passed over several senior Merck executives who were considered contenders for the top job." Though unexpected, Gilmartin's appointment received a warm reception from Wall Street, where Merck's stock was sent soaring.

If the announcement of Gilmartin's move to Merck was a surprise to Wall Street and close observers of the company, it was a shock to those at BD, most especially to the board. "Our board was stunned," recalls John Galiardo, then and now the company's general counsel. "We hadn't paid much attention to succession planning; Ray was only fifty at the time. We thought he would continue as CEO for many years."

It certainly was not Gilmartin's intention to throw BD into a tailspin with the announcement of his rapid departure; he was forced to keep talks with Merck confidential until the final offer came through. Merck was under considerable pressure to name a successor to longtime CEO Dr. P. Roy Vagelos, who was on record as saying that he wished to retire when he turned sixty-five, fewer than six months away at the time Gilmartin was appointed. Now, with the offer accepted by Gilmartin, Merck was eager to alleviate any anxiety about succession in the business community by announcing their decision immediately and getting Gilmartin on board as soon as possible.

With word out about Gilmartin's appointment, BD was suddenly in the midst of a crisis itself, and wasted no time in scheduling conference calls between Gilmartin and key directors to select a new CEO who would be ready to take over immediately. "To be honest," says Galiardo, who was not appointed to the board until after Gilmartin's departure, "directors were horrified at the news. Merck was announcing Gilmartin's appointment right away, and [BD] directors were sort of pissed to be put in that position [about having to respond on such short notice with their own CEO successor announcement]."

Though BD's board had never formally decided on an immediate replacement for Gilmartin should he leave suddenly, Clateo Castellini, president of BD's Private Medical Sector, was the obvious and natural choice. For some time Gilmartin had made it clear that Castellini was his number one choice as a successor, a preference he reiterated to the board when discussing his departure and replacement with them. The only problem was that Castellini, then in his late fifties, had already announced that he planned to retire, voluntarily, within a short time. He had remained an Italian national and wanted to return to Italy and enjoy himself after a long and successful career.

Castellini was in Asia at the time of Merck's announcement, and the board contacted him to see if he would be willing to postpone his retirement and serve as Gilmartin's successor. He accepted the offer and was quickly approved by the board. Though Castellini was perhaps not a long-term succession solution for BD because of his age, he had proven himself as a highly capable leader within the company. In the wake of Merck's announcement BD's directors wanted to avoid, if at all possible, not being able to announce a replacement for Gilmartin.

Though he had built an impressive career with BD, Castellini had

had no prior board experience whatever, at his own company or elsewhere, when he was tapped as their next CEO. This presented a significant challenge for him as he moved, literally on a moment's notice, from an operating role to management of the governance of the company. Castellini was fortunate in having the assistance of general counsel, John Galiardo, who was made vice chairman, appointed to the board, and was able to pave the way for Castellini to develop a working relationship with the board of directors.

It is far from ideal for an individual to be thrust into the CEO spot with little or no board experience, as Castellini was. For that reason, we strongly recommend that, as part of the seasoning and education of potential successors, companies encourage them to round out their operating experience with some board experience. With fewer insiders on boards these days it is generally not considered wise to have an internal successor on the board, but in our opinion they should be urged to serve on outside boards. In that way, whether or not the timing of the succession goes exactly as planned, successors will be as well prepared to contribute their expertise in the boardroom as they are to the company's operations.

Gilmartin's abrupt departure and the rapid-fire decisions that had to be made regarding the appointment of a successor have had a chastening effect on BD's board. As a result, they are now a little less cavalier when it comes to succession planning, and have implemented a much more formal process, particularly since Castellini will undoubtedly be planning for his own retirement in the not too distant future. It would seem that there will be fewer surprises this time around no matter what the circumstances when Castellini ultimately exits the company.

BD's board now devotes a full session exclusively to succession-related matters one to two times a year. During these sessions Castellini carefully reviews all candidates for higher office and the board has the opportunity to ask extensive questions regarding abilities and additional experience candidates will need to add to round out their portfolios. Having been in the hot seat once, the board is acutely aware of the importance of being kept fully informed about all potential successors. Says Galiardo, "Ray thought carefully about succession, but it wasn't handled with the rigor we now handle it with. I doubt that we'll ever let up on succession planning as a result of the trauma after Ray's departure. . . . We would never want the shock of a CEO leaving to tank our stock price."

IBM: The Need for a Clean Sweep

As Merck's hiring of Raymond Gilmartin illustrates, more boards seem to be looking outside their company for a CEO. What motivates an outside search? It may mean that the company has not done its homework in breeding internal candidates, or that an industry is in the throes of rapid and far-reaching change, meaning no insiders are well equipped to deal with the new challenges. A failed strategy may have led to a dwindling share price that threatens to ignite an angry shareholder reaction. All of these situations may necessitate the search for an outside successor.

It is important to keep in mind that board members represent shareholders, and shareholders need the assurance that the company is pursuing a sound strategy. If a company is suffering losses, declining share price, bad media, or other problems, shareholders may conclude not only that the CEO isn't right for the company but that the strategy isn't either. In that case a board may conclude that the removal of the CEO is not enough to address the uncertainty and ease shareholder concerns. A new direction may be called for, and an outsider may be needed to implement it, even if the company's executive ranks offer a cadre of experienced leaders. When such strategic changes entail restructuring and major cuts in employees, many companies assume (and the facts bear them out) that it is harder for an insider than an outsider to mobilize the company and implement the needed degree of change. Moreover, rightly or wrongly, internal successors may be viewed as tainted by virtue of their association with a CEO who is perceived as a failure.

Sometimes a decision to bypass the internal team in favor of an outsider is a way for a company to make a powerful statement about fundamental change. When IBM went outside to replace John Akers, the board was making just this sort of statement, and it passed over some substantial internal talent in its desire to make a clean break from Akers.

Between 1991 and 1993, under John F. Akers' leadership, IBM had lost more than $8 billion, cut its stock dividend for the first time, and began its first-ever layoffs. The continuing poor results prompted tremendous pressure from institutional investors, analysts, and the media to depose a legendary CEO and bring in new leadership to turn the company around. A week after IBM posted a staggering $4.97 billion net loss for 1992, the board announced that Akers would be replaced after eight years as CEO and more than thirty years with the company. On the same day that Akers' departure was announced, shareholders—who had seen their investment shrink by 64 percent during his tenure—were told their dividend was to be cut by 55 percent.

With Akers' seat open, a number of high-profile insiders, including Michael Armstrong, senior vice president and chairman, president, and CEO, IBM World Trade Corporation (who would go on to serve as CEO at Hughes Electronics and AT&T), faced off against each other in a classic horse race. But despite a top-management team of several talented and experienced senior executives, the board decided it had to go outside the company. Going outside allowed the company to send a clear message to shareholders and the public that they were determined to infuse truly fresh leadership into the computer giant. And so the board chose Louis V. Gerstner, CEO of RJR Nabisco, Inc. (former president of American Express and, earlier, director of McKinsey), a leader known as a brilliant strategist but one with no experience in the world of computing technology.

Going outside IBM in this situation required sacrifices. Some outstanding insiders, including Michael Armstrong, were passed over and ultimately lost to the company. But the drop in share value was a powerful force in the decision-making process, one that was ultimately too strong to ignore. Shareholders needed a symbol of change, and the board had little choice but to provide it if it was to maintain investor confidence in the company going forward.

Eastman Kodak: Shareholders Demand a Say

The process to replace Akers at IBM is not the only example of the growing power of large institutional investors. Indeed, in recent years large shareholder groups worried about the value of their investments have forced the ouster of a number of longtime CEOs of large public companies. When the stock price slips, and the CEO does not respond quickly enough with a plan to repair the damage with needed changes in the company, the solution is often to replace the CEO with someone who will take immediate action.

Kay R. Whitmore, then CEO of Kodak, learned that in August 1993. An engineer, Whitmore had joined Kodak in 1957. After 33 years he reached the top of the company, taking over as CEO in 1990. But Whitmore's tenure as CEO was challenging. Large shareholders, anxious to see increased profits, were demanding big cost cuts and were impatient at the pace with which Whitmore was pursuing them. At a meeting with large shareholding institutions in the summer of 1993 he tried to reassure them, pointing out that he was planning to bring down a restructuring plan scheduled for the fall. But as the *Washington Post* described it: "When most of the group supported the proposal to lay off 20,000 workers and sell the company's Sterling Winthrop drug unit, Whitmore said his own plan would not be nearly so aggressive."

Nine days later the board voted to replace Whitmore as chairman, president, and CEO, rather than wait for his restructuring plan to be unveiled. They issued a statement that read: "We believe there is a clear need to move faster and further on operating cost efficiencies and enhanced earnings." While the board ultimately acknowledged Whitmore's success at reducing debt, they had evidently grown impatient with the pace in boosting profits.

Where did the board look for a solution to Kodak's leadership problem? Under the circumstances, the board looked outside. Two months after the announcement of Whitmore's departure, the company announced the hiring of George M. C. Fisher, chairman and chief executive of Motorola, Inc. The timing could not have been more symbolic. Fisher's appointment came only hours after Kodak had announced a loss of $68 million in the third quarter as a result of a huge restructuring charge.

As the *Post* described it, Whitmore was a victim of the "national revolt of shareholders and outside directors." His dismissal was a symbol of a newfound aggressiveness that is changing the nature of CEO hirings and firings, and enhancing the importance of CEO succession as a priority for corporate boards.

Hercules: Succession Planning by the Book

When a longtime, highly respected CEO stays on track to planned retirement, succession planning looks entirely different from that which catches boards by surprise and must be accomplished rapidly in a crisis atmosphere. When Thomas L. Gossage completed the final phase of his retirement from Hercules, Inc., in January 1997, it was the finishing touch to a carefully planned and executed succession.

Those who were not aware of all the behind-the-scenes planning may have viewed the CEO transition as a case of a successful CEO merely handpicking his successor. This view would not only be wrong, it also would display a complete lack of understanding of Hercules' board, which, for good reason, has been recognized on more than one occasion—in *Business Week,* for example—as one of the best boards in America. The board works with the CEO but does not answer to him. In succession planning as in other areas of board responsibility, directors want to avoid "management capture" at all costs. And while Hercules' directors give prime consideration to the CEO's recommendation, they don't necessarily defer to it.

The directors' modus operandi came as no surprise to former Hercules CEO Thomas L. Gossage, who knew from day one what a strong and independent board he would be working with. In 1990, Hercules' board had rejected the first recommendation of Gossage's predecessor, and appointed Gossage CEO instead.

When Gossage stepped down as CEO (remaining as chairman) in 1997, the board approved his choice as successor, Keith Elliott, who had joined Hercules in 1990 after nine years at Engelhard Corporation in various financial positions. But the directors' decision was based on due diligence, not undue deference. "The board has a great deal of confidence in the CEO, but we have a strong board and the role of the directors is to challenge the CEO's opinion," says Edward Carrington, the company's former VP of human resources.

Long before a vacancy is expected to occur, directors are continually provided information about the potential candidates, the chance to get to know them, and the opportunity to track their progress within the company. The succession process comprises a number of other critical steps:

- *At an annual dinner with the board, the CEO evaluates inside candidates and their readiness to succeed to his position.* The board also expects the CEO to present other candidates who may be ready to assume the top position according to a longer time frame (three to five years), and to describe what is being done to help them broaden their array of skills and experience. "It was interesting to me as we went through the process how people would grow and change in their assessments," says Edith Holiday, who serves on the board of Hercules and several other companies. "Someone who was a less likely candidate for a top spot one year could be more likely the following year depending on his performance."

- *The board insists at all times on one "ready now" or "drop-in" candidate*—someone who could step in and fill the CEO's shoes on a moment's notice in the event of a sudden need—and will always want the CEO and other top managers to demonstrate that they are "two deep" in any position.

- *Since Hercules strictly limits the number of insiders on its board, the company has created a management advisory board*—which includes the executive vice presidents (business heads), the chief legal counsel, and the chief financial officer—to provide the top-management team with exposure to outside directors as well a more global view of the business. This management group sits in on board meetings (although the board can ask them to leave), giving directors the opportunity to tap management's expertise without risking slipping into the role of actually managing the company rather than overseeing its management.

• *The amount of time spent on succession preparation is based on the imminence of the CEO's retirement.* If the CEO is planning to retire in the near future, every board meeting would include a roughly hour-long closed session regarding progress on a successor. Directors would want to know exactly what the CEO is doing to ensure a smooth transition and what they would need to do. As he approached retirement, Gossage not only discussed likely candidates for top positions at the annual dinner but also updated the board in executive sessions of outside directors after each board meeting (held eight times a year).

• *If the situation is less urgent, the once-a-year board meeting might suffice.* "In such a case, the emphasis would not be on rehashing candidates, but on reviewing development plans against potential candidates in order to force an internal development discussion," explains Carrington.

• *As part of the grooming process for a CEO candidate, directors might introduce him or her to people they know outside the company who could serve as mentors in various areas.*

When it came to succession, Hercules' CEO and board had clearly done their homework, but one should not confuse thoroughness with predictability. As Holiday recalls, Gossage "shuffled the deck of top reports about four times. It was stressful for those involved—they would be pulled out of one assignment and into another—but purposeful. He would test people out by, for example, putting someone who couldn't make decisions into a line job where he had to make decisions and see what happened. He would try to get the most out of every person and, as a result of the experience, everyone felt they had a go at it [the CEO position]."

Gossage also made sure that directors knew their views were a crucial part of the decision-making process. "The way he presented it to the board wasn't 'Keith's the guy you've got to take,' but 'here's why I think he's good,'" Holiday says.

About a year before Gossage retired, Elliott was appointed president and COO and took a seat on the board, with Gossage remaining as chairman and CEO. "That was a 'look-see,'" says Holiday, "a chance for us to watch Keith closely in that role. It was a test drive—when directors had a chance to ask themselves, 'Is this going to work? Let's find out now.'"

The Hercules board's ultimate approval of Elliott was based on a process that was long on careful planning and short on unpleasant surprises. Of course, the company was fortunate in that regard. They had a CEO who was in good health, was not wooed away by another company, and did not incur antagonism from shareholders. But it is important to give credit where credit is due: to an outstanding board that has proven time and time again to be a capable and thoughtful partner to the CEO, one that carefully assesses all options before determining what is in the best interest of the company.

Cigna: When a CEO Is Far from the Retirement Zone

When Wilson "Bill" Taylor assumed the position of CEO of Cigna Corporation a decade ago at the young age of forty-four, one might not have expected him to make planning for his successor a high priority. But Taylor's philosophy is straightforward: When it comes to the important task of ensuring a trained successor is ready to take his place, the age of the CEO is irrelevant.

"You still have to plan for the emergencies that may arise," says Taylor, "illness or death, the CEO may leave for another company. Whatever the CEO's age, even if he's a brand-new CEO and only forty-five, you still have to plan for those expected situations. And if you think about it, there are very few people who start at a relatively young age and say, 'I know I'll be here for twenty years, therefore we can skip a generation.' Planning for succession goes on in much the same fashion, though maybe not with the same sense of urgency."

Indeed, it is hardly unheard of for CEOs to die suddenly or leave rather abruptly for new opportunities, as with Gilmartin at Becton,

Dickinson. Considering this uncertainty combined with the gener-ally shorter tenure of CEOs, companies are increasingly aware that there is no predicting how long a CEO will remain in his or her position.

In view of what he considered uncontrollable variables and his longer-term agenda, Taylor made succession planning, particularly the management development, a regular part of his and the board's agenda. "In our case, I have a major targeted discussion with the board annually regarding possible successors. Even though there is only a remote possibility that something could happen to me, they know who the alternatives would be in case of an emergency. The board gets my evaluation of successors, and annually I record my opinion. I talk with the board in detail about the two or three people inside who could replace me, and we carefully evaluate the strengths and weaknesses of each. Though it is a topic we touch on regularly at board meetings, the in-depth discussion is once a year.

"Afterward, I put suggestions and evaluations in a letter to the head of our People Resources Committee marked 'to be opened in the event of my death or disability.' The reasons for the letter are sim-ple. Even though I may already have discussed my suggestions with the board, suppose eight months later I die in a plane crash. Does everyone remember exactly what you said? The letter represents only what I would suggest. It's a free-floating thing and it changes contin-ually, depending on the readiness of successors and business condi-tions. There's nothing mysterious about this process and, ultimately, of course it's the board's decision. This represents my best advice and it's one piece of input they have before they would have to come to a decision."

When a CEO is far from the retirement zone and is performing well with no plans to move on in sight, the succession focus is chiefly on the management-development process. "We give a lot of thought to, and expend a lot of effort on, our regular development process, to identifying who are the best longer-term successors. When I work with the board, we are continually evaluating our progress: Are we paying enough attention to management development? Are people getting enough training, enough experience? Are we paying enough attention to people other than possible immediate successors—to business heads and people coming up who would have CEO potential?"

One thing, according to Taylor, that is important to recognize when the CEO is relatively young is that the leading succession candidates are more likely to change over what is probably a greater span of time. "We ask ourselves, 'Among the senior players, who are the leading prospects? What do we need to do for their development?' But we are well aware that some of the direct reports are unlikely to be successors because of their age and the amount of time involved before we would make a change. So perhaps we focus even more than some other companies on the next level down, on the younger managers getting the attention and experience they need to develop. At this level there is still time to make a material difference." And that is where Cigna's CEO and board concentrate much of their energy when it comes to succession planning.

Board Checklist

Given that directors bear the ultimate responsibility for ensuring an orderly succession with a CEO who can best meet a company's needs at a particular time, what can a board do to replace a false sense of security with a real one? This chapter reveals several steps boards should take:

1. Boards must adopt the proper mind-set: Remember, no one is immortal, and there is no guarantee that a CEO will remain with the company until retirement.
2. Boards should expect to be apprised by the CEO on a regular basis about potential successors, and their stage of leadership development. In the event of a sudden need for a new CEO, this information will enable the board make an informed decision regarding a successor.
3. Boards should know the potential candidates well, and have a sense of how they perform in a wide range of situations. That means directors should expect access to top-level

management, and the opportunity to see them perform in board meetings and social settings.

4. Directors should plan for the worst—assume that a CEO may suffer an unexpected health problem, recognize that a CEO may well accept an offer from another company, or that for some other reason he or she may have to be replaced quickly—and plan for those contingencies.

5. The CEO should continually keep the board advised of a recommended "drop-in" candidate in case a successor were to be needed immediately. This is a key practice and one that all companies should make an integral part of their succession process.

Whatever the succession scenario that ultimately plays out, companies that have planned carefully will be able to respond quickly and wisely under any of a range of circumstances, allowing them to maintain a calm posture among investors, employees, and customers. Having a well-developed process in place long before any successor has to be announced is half the battle, and the greatest advocates of this careful planning, as we have seen, are those companies that have been forced to wing it when a CEO departs suddenly. More about developing the process and implementing it in the next chapter, "Putting a Process in Place."

3

Putting a Process in Place

"The trick is to formulate solutions that meet more than one scenario, can be changed quickly, and allow you to move fast when you have to, like Wayne Gretsky skating to where the puck is going to be, or a chess player seeing two or three moves ahead in the game. These scenarios require an infinite number of alternatives and require flexibility and agility."

—Raymond Smith, former CEO, Bell Atlantic Corporation

Prior to his departure as the CEO of Bell Atlantic in 1998, Ray Smith had developed two inside candidates, and through the acquisition of Nynex a third emerged as the successor. Smith's choice—against the backdrop of the merger and turbulence in the industry—reflected his recognition of the need to link strategy and succession planning.

Though the quote from Smith was made specifically about corporate strategy, it couldn't be more germane to the succession-planning process, which, as we will discuss, begins with an analysis of strategy. We've already established that succession can follow any one of a range of scenarios, depending on the particular circumstances and culture of a given company. Likewise, when it comes to process, there is no one "right" way of doing things that can be stamped from a mold and superimposed on a company. In this case, one size definitely does not fit all. A key characteristic of succession planning, in fact, is that there must be a great deal of built-in flexibility. Whatever form the succession process may take at an individual company, however, there are recognizable elements that best-practice companies we have observed seem to share. Highlighting these elements or basic principles as they relate to the succession process is what this chapter is all about.

The Payoff of Good Process

It is important to note that the succession process is not merely a means to an end—the proper selection of a new CEO. The process itself, not just the ultimate outcome, is important for the following reasons:

- *Cleansing the organization.* If undertaken in an open and objective manner, and with the input of global intelligence® (an ongoing inventory and assessment of management resources both inside and outside the company), the process can free the organization from much of the inevitable infighting and politics.

- *Communicating fairness.* The process should leave all contenders, successful or unsuccessful, with the feeling that they had a fair shot at the CEO position.

- *Legitimizing outcome.* A process that is perceived by all in the company to be fair lends legitimacy to the winner and makes it possible for him or her to lead if the general feeling is that all major constituencies had a voice in the process.

Another important point to make up front about the succession process is that we define "process" as an ongoing phenomenon, a measured response to a particular challenge that entails proper planning, as opposed to a transaction or event that may take place in a crisis atmosphere. Carefully and thoughtfully pursued, the succession process can fulfill several long-term goals: It can help develop and clarify strategy for the future, benchmark top-level human resources against the rest of the corporate world, and generate an ongoing wellspring of executive talent that can meet a company's leadership needs on an ongoing basis.

Marrying Succession to Business Strategy

No succession process proceeds in a vacuum. It is closely linked to other critical corporate processes, particularly the determination of strategy. Well-planned successions, in fact, start with a thorough delineation of business strategy, which then serves as a road map for the rest of the process. And as the company's strategy shifts over time, so should the roster and ranking of likely successors. The science and art of selecting the most capable successor to the CEO has more to do with a vision of the company for the future—and finding a leader who will be capable of bringing that vision to fruition—than its assessment of the past or even the present.

In selecting a CEO, a company must look not just at the business environment in which it has traditionally operated, but also at the ways in which it is changing. Deregulation, technological advances, new competitors, and shifting markets are among many factors that can require a company to overhaul its business strategy. Similarly, such factors must be taken into account in the selection of the CEO who will best be able to deal with them.

Given the vast and far-reaching changes in telecommunications, it is not surprising that companies in that industry make it a priority to attempt to forecast future scenarios, and then to find a leader who will best be able to deal with them. Ray Smith, former CEO of Bell Atlantic, offers some perspective on the accelerated pace of change, particularly in an industry driven by innovation:

"In our short fifteen-year life span," Smith says of Bell Atlantic, "we've seen more change than the old Bell system saw in a hundred years.... When I started at the old telephone company, I received five promotions in five years, basically for being lucid, cogent, and showing up regularly. During that time absolutely nothing happened, nothing changed. . . . Now every single day we get more clippings about our industry—whatever on earth that is—than we truly did in those first five years. . . ."

Such a fast-changing business climate requires a company to look ahead and to continually reassess the skills and attributes required to lead it in what may be a radically different business environment.

"There are a thousand different scenarios for how changing technology and regulation and customer behavior will play out," says Smith. "We can't predict one; we don't have business plans that are set that way. All of these alternative futures are all plausible, they're all possible, and they must be planned for—every single one of them—but they won't all happen, only one will happen." How then does a company shape a business strategy that manages both to keep ahead of change and steer clear of devastating risks? Smith calls for a combination of speed, dexterity, and foresight.

Smith's comments on strategy and leadership development make clear why a company's strategic goals and its choice of CEO are inextricably linked. In the planning phases, both processes focus on identifying specific needs and opportunities, then on exploring and developing a number of potential solutions, so that when it comes time to sign off on a specific strategic goal or CEO successor, a board is in a position to activate what it views as the most effective solution.

Boards and CEOs must do more than focus narrowly on internal leadership criteria—personal traits related to how an individual has performed as a leader compared to others in the company. The frame of reference must be much larger: Boards must attempt to predict how effective the contenders will be in achieving the business strategy articulated by the board. With the world changing so rapidly around them, boards cannot risk evaluating potential leaders in a vacuum. As part of the board's "due diligence" in the succession process, finding the best successor increasingly means a thorough analysis of prospects not only in a variety of functional roles, but also with some indication of how well they have performed under circumstances the company is likely to face in the future.

Finding a CEO to Advance the Strategy

Donald Frey knows something about being both a CEO and a director. The former CEO of Bell & Howell Company has a total of eighty-six years of service on ten boards. He has been through seventeen CEO successions, including eight that he helped to carry out as a director, seeing "everything from disasters to noble results to everything in between." He believes that the critical first step in selecting a future leader is the articulation of the company's future direction. That means that the board of directors must play an active role.

"The problem with most discussion about succession," Frey explains, "is that it's anecdotal, and it's done after the fact. . . . The board needs to be questioning, 'What kind of a CEO do we want?' If you pick a clone of the CEO, the implication is that life will continue on more like the past than different, and that's a prediction you can't make today."

Both from the point of view of responsibility and acceptance of outcome, Frey emphasizes that the succession process must be managed by directors. "It's not the sitting CEO's responsibility to pick his successor; in the final analysis it's the board's responsibility."

An additional reason for the board to control succession is to ensure that the process is seen as fair. Frey observes that when a CEO handpicks the successor, and fails to recognize his or her "number one" assistant and logical successor, both the CEO and the company will suffer serious repercussions in terms of loyalty, even if the decision was made on the basis of the future needs of the company.

Since a company will be attempting to identify and prepare capable successors who are compatible with its strategy, the process will not be accomplished overnight and should not be undertaken at the last minute. The board should be exploring the process a good eighteen months to two years before the planned retirement of a current company leader. If the succession is being completed according to a planned retirement scenario—rather than a sudden crisis—the CEO should certainly have ample time to discuss the future direction of the company with the board, and an outside consultant if appropriate. "The process starts with discussion, lots of discussion," Frey says. "Strategy first, and then who we want to carry out the strategy: the person's style, background, and record."

Internal vs. External?

The need to address strategic goals and find leaders who are able to propel them forward is one of the reasons why Ray Smith believes companies, as part of their search, should at least examine the world-wide market for executive talent.

"We've got to change our traditional approach to growing executive talent inside the business," Smith said in a 1998 presentation at an AESC conference. "The main reason is that we simply don't have the time for the typical fifteen- to twenty-year gestation period for career development to produce the kind of leader that looks exactly like us." No longer, he says, should going outside for a key executive be "viewed as a failure of internal processes."

Smith's comments notwithstanding, currently only a small percentage of companies go outside for leaders. Indeed, when Smith stepped down after negotiating a merger with GTE, his successor as designated co-CEO was Ivan Seidenberg, promoted from within Bell Atlantic. Similarly, the process in the vast majority of companies will result in the naming of an internal successor. Even today there is a deep-seated cultural prejudice against going outside the company for a new leader. CEOs, directors, and top human resources executives at most of the best-practice companies we interviewed expressed the belief that a company that must go outside to select a new CEO has failed at one of its most basic and important duties, that of developing capable, ongoing leadership.

The tendency to hire and promote from within may be shifting, however, particularly as industries that have been overhauled by rapid and far-reaching change find that reaching outside is the only way to get the leadership skills and experience they need to survive. For example, if a board believes that the CEO is ill equipped to provide guidance across the new terrain, it is not likely to have confidence that a key member of the CEO's team will be any more capable of dealing with a turnaround situation.

Whether a company is firmly committed to selecting its next leader from its own ranks or going outside, we strongly believe that it is the board's responsibility, at the very least, to scan the market for leadership talent. This panoramic approach is part of the board's due diligence in carrying out its most important responsibility: assuring that it has helped identify and secure the most capable future leader for the company.

What an Outside Consultant Can Contribute

As companies increasingly view succession as a more complex process than merely filling a vacancy—especially if they are committed to scanning the universe outside—they may find it necessary to work with a consultant who can provide not only the intelligence but also the analysis. We work with clients seeking internal successors as well as those who want to at least consider leaders who are available outside their company. In much the way that McKinsey's & Co.'s advice is sought on strategy and Towers Perrins' is sought on compensation, we consult with clients on succession matters. Consistent with the theme of this chapter, the most effective way to utilize a consulting firm is not just to deal with a crisis, but also to help put in place and monitor a process that will avoid crisis. If a board is going to engage a consulting firm to help deal with succession issues, the ideal time to start is before a vacancy occurs.

What should consultants be expected to bring to the process? They should help to ensure a positive outcome by providing experience and expertise geared to best succession practices, including:

- expanding the point of view of major decision makers, including directors and the CEO, by syndicating the experiences of many companies, including particular challenges and solutions;

- helping a company understand the options that lie ahead regarding succession planning and what may be the best way to go;

- benchmarking, according to objective criteria, the capabilities of likely internal candidates against comparable leaders both inside and outside the industry;

- ensuring, if a company does have to go outside for its successor, that a range of solutions is considered, including the more obvious choices as well as less likely, more creative options, especially when a very different type of leader is required because of rapid change within the industry.

While the depth of a consultant's involvement will vary depending on the particular client situation, a good consultant will encourage the client to at least consider all of the elements that contribute to a good process. Not only is the final result likely to be superior to a more haphazard approach, but also the board will have the added peace of mind of knowing that its choice was based on careful, deliberate decision making, which it should also be able to document.

MetLife's CMO: An Incubator for Future CEOs

Catherine Rein, currently senior executive vice president, Business Services Group, Corporate Services, and formerly senior vice president of human resources for Metropolitan Life Insurance Company, states the company's basic philosophy when it comes to succession: "to take as much of the human drama out of succession planning as possible." Instead of making it a cliff-hanger, the goal is to make it as predictable a process as possible. MetLife pursues that goal by maintaining an ongoing process that nurtures, evaluates, and provides a platform for the company's extended management team. In the following section we analyze the various components of MetLife's unique succession process.

- *The process includes a vehicle to provide the CEO and the board with a comprehensive picture of the company's top management team.*

That picture is developed through annual and semiannual organization reviews during which some fifty MetLife executives are evaluated. The company has conducted such reviews as far back as MetLife's former CEO, Harry Kamen (who retired in 1998 but remains on the board), can remember; they became more formalized in 1993, with Kamen's ascension to chairman and CEO from senior executive vice president. Each spring, the top ten to twelve executives—known collectively as the Corporate Management Office (CMO)—outline plans for their own succession and for development of their management team. This includes an assessment of executives one level below them, whence the senior VPs' successors will come, highlighting high-potential succession candidates that the CEO and the board should be aware of.

In the fall the CEO briefs the directors on the review's results, showcasing the talent of high-potential executives. In this way the organization review maintains an ongoing dialogue between the management team and the board, continually assessing the capabilities of the management team and its individual members.

- *The process ensures that continual attention is paid to CEO succession.*

One segment of the organization review is devoted exclusively to that topic; indeed, it becomes the center of discussion twice a year when the CEO is approaching retirement. At one such meeting with the board not long before his retirement, Kamen says, "I discussed who I viewed as the strongest candidates to succeed me as CEO, and evaluated each one's strengths and weaknesses." At the next meeting with the board, Kamen focused on a reduced number of potential successors.

- *The process includes institutionalized structures to train and assess immediate candidates for CEO.*

One such structure is the CMO, which is actively involved in all aspects of the CEO's decision making, meeting weekly. In addition to giving the CEO access to a wide range of views, the CMO creates a broad leadership base. In the event of a crisis that would render the CEO unable to serve, the CMO group could step into his shoes on a moment's notice.

As Kamen puts it, the CMO is "a way to build better CEOs." It gives potential successors not just the opportunity to be exposed to the CEO's decision making, but also to participate in it. Of course, there are two sides to the looking glass; the CEO has an opportunity to observe the top-management team at close range, shaping informed recommendations to the board regarding a successor.

- *The process provides growth opportunities to help developing managers become executive leaders.*

Feeding into the pipeline to top management is the Executive Council—the group of sixty managers below the top twelve that comprise the CMO—which meets quarterly. Another structure that keeps the emphasis at MetLife on developing managers who will one day be capable executive leaders comprises the thirty cross-department teams that the company has created as the final phase of a total corporate reengineering effort. The teams, which have some ten members each, and are advised by two members of the CMO, expose more than three hundred managers and officers, at all levels, to a variety of critical aspects of the business.

In spite of the great emphasis on internal management development, MetLife is not an insular organization. When required to strengthen their bench, they occasionally bring in outsiders at the executive VP level, including Gary A. Beller, executive vice president and chief legal officer, in 1994. The infusion of an outside perspective is most notable, however, in their "window on the world" approach to assessing their seniormost managers, in which they benchmark internal candidates for senior management positions by comparing them to those in similar positions on the outside. "To assure ourselves that we have the best person, we have to look around and see what's out there," says Kamen. "By benchmarking those in senior positions, we can get a more accurate picture of how we really look on the inside."

"Our goal is to develop our own talent," adds Rein, "but the periodic outside check also serves as a frame of reference."

MetLife's "active, no-nonsense" board is also a critical element in the succession-planning process. This has not always been the case. When Kamen became the company's corporate secretary in 1979, he was instrumental in helping to revamp the corporate-governance process. As a result of these changes, the board has taken on a much more active role in overseeing MetLife's business. "I present things to them in an orderly way, and they start cross-examining me," Kamen, a lawyer by training, says affectionately. The CEO and the board are obviously in synch on a number of things where the best interests of the company are concerned, including on matters related to succession planning. The board insists on a "rational, organized, reasoned" succession process, and this is obviously an area of the highest priority for the CEO.

How does the composition of the board affect succession planning? Both Kamen and Rein agree that the actual board structure doesn't much matter; what is significant is that directors have experience with big companies and the myriad complex issues that confront them. "Current or former CEOs with this background understand the issues inside out. They can push you by asking the right questions." says Kamen.

What does it take to make the succession-planning process work? First of all, says Kamen, the CEO must be truly committed to making it work. The formal process, and corresponding deadlines, now that it is in place, helps, because it "disciplines you to take the time." The board must not only understand its critical role in the process but also be willing to push for feedback and the action needed to keep the process flowing smoothly. When MetLife's board is presented with annual reviews of promising managers in the company, they urge top managers to define development programs designed to broaden the experience of these executives, to assure an uninterrupted flow of developing leadership.

Another practice that contributes to successful succession planning is the fact that the board's nominating and compensation committee, which overseas the organizational review/succession planning process, links a significant percentage of the CEO's long-term incentive compensation to how well that person meets his or her goals regarding succession planning. Even though in the case of a dedicated CEO such as Kamen this mechanism may not be needed, it is still best to have it in place.

With all of its emphasis on internal development, when it came time to announce a successor to Kamen in March 1998, the company announced that it had named Robert H. Benmosche, a relative newcomer to MetLife who had built his career in the securities industry. Considering the radical transformation the insurance industry has been undergoing as part of the overall consolidation of financial services, the choice of a successor with vast experience in business areas that represented MetLife's future, rather than its present or past, did not come as much of a surprise to observers.

In its announcement of the succession decision, the *Wall Street Journal* noted: "The naming of Mr. Benmosche represents a break with MetLife's historic practice of promoting a long-time insider to the top job and comes as other insurers including Prudential Life Insurance Company of America have looked outside for leaders. MetLife, Prudential and other conventional life insurers face heightened competition for consumers' savings from the securities and mutual-fund industries."

The selection of Kamen's successor demonstrates MetLife's determination not to be left in the dust as the industry and the very definition of a life insurance company go through dramatic overhauls. Benmosche, who joined MetLife in 1995 after fourteen years at PaineWebber, Inc., said in an interview that his promotion is a sign of the insurance industry's determination to compete effectively in selling all sorts of financial products, from conventional life insurance products to mutual funds.

The selection of Benmosche was a wise and forward-thinking solution for this particular company at this particular time. In essence, MetLife's board arrived at a succession decision that represents the best of both worlds. Since Benmosche had already spent several years as an insider, he had been tested and had succeeded at MetLife. Yet he also brought a fresh perspective to the company and was prepared as CEO to move aggressively into new areas dictated by the strategy the board delineated for the company. In short, the board determined the company's future direction, then decided that Benmosche was best suited to execute that strategy based on the skill set he brought to the table.

Most important, the succession planning process at MetLife is successful because it is not strictly geared toward accomplishing a task— finding a successor to the CEO. Rather, succession planning is one element, albeit a key one, of the company's organizational development process. The entire process is an organic and ongoing one, not transaction-related, in which there is a regular and continual exposure of candidates for positions, at all levels, who are making their way up the ranks and who will be needed to infuse fresh blood into the ranks of top management.

Thermo Electron: Process Takes Precedence in a Family-Owned Company

"Thermo Electron may not be the mother of all companies," says Hoover's, Inc., publisher of company profiles, "but it is the parent or grandparent of a brood of publicly traded, technology-related subsidiaries." Though it is now in the process of scaling back, the parent had some twenty-three offspring in its orbit when George Hatsopoulos first consulted us in early 1999 about a particularly challenging succession situation. While the situation Thermo Electron faced was of a magnitude most companies, even large conglomerates, are unlikely to face, there is much that can be learned from this example about the value of good process.

In the case of Thermo Electron, central leadership and governance are critical, even though the individual businesses are far-flung as well as highly independent and entrepreneurial. There was a great deal of concern about finding a replacement CEO capable of effectively leveraging the company's unique culture and structure. Replacing an owner/founder can be notoriously difficult. When the successor must be intimately familiar with, in this case, just shy of two dozen "children," there are not likely to be many candidates up to the task.

In addition to these broad challenges facing him and his company, Hatsopoulos was concerned about a number of related challenges when we first met:

- Increasingly, there were concerns, both internally and externally, about Thermo Electron's long-term strategy.

- While there was a notable lack of consensus among key insiders regarding internal successors, there were several business unit heads who would be crucial for the company to retain going forward.

- The unique culture of Thermo Electron had not proven hospitable in the past to the occasional introduction of outside senior-level talent.

- The company's $4 billion business portfolio involved diverse product lines, so success and expertise in one area did not necessarily translate to another. Consequently there had been little cross-pollination of senior managers across businesses, and no one executive was clearly qualified to provide overarching leadership for the entire enterprise.

- Wall Street was following succession plans at Thermo Electron with more than casual interest, particularly in light of the company's recent difficulties.

The task, then, was to find a replacement for founder/CEO George Hatsopoulos, whose vision and drive for technological innovation had permeated the company since its inception. The new CEO would have to possess a range and depth of skills not ordinarily found in one individual: strong leadership ability, strategic vision, and technical competence.

Confronted by this awesome challenge, Hatsopoulos's instinct was to let a systematic and solid process lead the way. It is never easy for someone who has built and led a successful business to step aside for the next generation of leadership. But Hatsopoulos recognized that focusing on an objective process with clearly defined criteria and benchmarks was the most reliable way to identify a capable successor and help ensure a successful future for the company.

From the start of our involvement with Thermo Electron it was evident that Hatsopoulos would take a leadership role in orchestrating the succession process and making sure the board had the information, advice, and perspective they would need to make an informed decision on whom they would ultimately select as the next CEO.

Our responsibility to gather the intelligence the board required for input into the decision-making process actually comprised three separate exercises:

- *interviewing and assessing the top 20 executives in the company,* with a particular focus on the four internal candidates who enjoyed varying degrees of support as potential CEO candidates;

- *benchmarking those internal candidates against potential outsiders* who could provide the board with perspective on the caliber of talent that might be attracted to the CEO role if they opted for an outside search;

- *interviewing and assessing, in depth, one outside director;* Dick Syron, who represented a possible compromise between selecting an insider and undertaking a search for a high-profile outsider, a process that could take up to six months to complete.

When we had completed the three phases of our assignment, we presented our conclusions and observations about the potential risks and opportunities of the various options to the board. In the end the board carefully weighed the issue of an insider versus an outsider. An insider would thoroughly understand Thermo Electron's complex and unique culture—clearly a key ingredient for success—yet none of the leading inside contenders was quite ready yet for the top job. An outsider with a "marquee" name could provide instant credibility with key constituencies as well as first-class management experience. But there was also a downside to this choice: An outsider would not have a feel for the idiosyncratic culture.

Ultimately the board selected director Dick Syron, who represented a best-of-both-worlds solution. As president of the American Stock Exchange, Syron clearly had the prestige and big-company management experience desired. As a member of Thermo Electron's board he also possessed a great deal of insight into the company's culture. A financially focused executive, Syron had helped to aggressively reshape the financial structure of Thermo Electron and develop a strategy for the company going forward. He had also helped to develop strong operating management, the group from which candidates would be drawn for both COO and CEO appointments within a three- to five-year time frame.

There is not necessarily anything remarkable about a board selecting a board member to step in as CEO. But it is remarkable that, given his attachment to and involvement in Thermo Electron, founder George Hatsopoulos was able to resist the emotional pull that so many owner/founders allow to override their reasoning when it comes to succession. Instead, Hatsopoulos chose to focus on a process that would allow the board to consider three well-thought-out and researched options. Particularly given the complexity of the task the CEO and the board faced, the approach Hatsopoulos chose will likely prove a critical step in the continued success of the company he worked so hard to build.

ContiGroup: A New Generation, a New Business

ContiGroup Companies, Inc. (formerly Continental Grain Company) is closely associated with a founding family but is a privately held, family-owned company. In this case, succession planning has its own peculiar challenges. Information about the company's performance may be less easily available, and developments with the company's leadership may be less often in the headlines, but a huge multinational such as ContiGroup can hardly hide from public view.

In the Fribourg family for five generations, ContiGroup made a couple of smooth and highly successful CEO transitions since 1994 when Michel Fribourg, an old-school entrepreneur, stepped down and was succeeded by Donald Staheli, who in turn was succeeded by Fribourg's son Paul in April 1997. The company has also gone through a transition of another kind, as it has moved far from its traditional roots to become an asset portfolio company. Staheli, a former meat industry executive, was the intermediary who bridged the transition when he succeeded the elder Fribourg as CEO and paved the way for the younger one to succeed him.

Succession at ContiGroup was far more than merely designating an heir. By just about any independent measure the younger Fribourg is an impressive and sophisticated financial executive. But no matter who you are at the company, even if—or perhaps especially if—your last name is Fribourg, you have to be able to get over the same hurdles as any other contender. The process determines the winner.

A major concern, which has helped to guide the succession planning process at ContiGroup and keep it on track, has been the ability of the company to continue to attract and hold on to the talented executives who will be so crucial to the ongoing success of the company. This focus, combined with the desire to combat the common perception that it may be hard to get to the top in a family-owned concern, have, if anything, resulted in a more rigorous succession process than at many public companies.

"Frankly," says Teresa McCaslin, executive vice president of human resources, "it can be very difficult to attract and retain top performers when there's a ceiling." To ensure that they are able to access and hold on to the best and the brightest, ContiGroup has implemented a systematic, ability-based succession planning process with identifiable, objective goals that is managed by a particularly strong and capable board working closely with the CEO and senior vice president of human resources. The overriding message, particularly with the board overseeing the process, is that those with superior ability who can contribute to the growth of the company are those who move up the ranks.

In fact, when Paul Fribourg was being considered for CEO, he had to compete with more potential candidates than Staheli had three years earlier. "We've tried to establish a less hierarchical, broader-based system where more senior executives are exposed to the broader issues affecting the company," Fribourg says. The key elements of that system include:

- *The company's seven-person management committee, directly involving all top-level executives in the management of the company.* "There's a great deal of opportunity for those on the management committee to exchange ideas rather than being stuck in the traditional silos," says McCaslin. The management committee consists of the presidents of the three operating divisions, the senior vice president for human resources, the senior vice president for investment and strategy, the chief legal counsel, and the vice chairman and CFO.

• *A great deal of ongoing board exposure to this top-management layer from which the successor to the CEO will most likely eventually come.* The board, in fact, interviewed all seven executives on the management committee before they were hired. Committee members make regular presentations to the board and have other opportunities to meet and socialize with them.

• *An operating committee, one level down from the management committee, is also a good grooming stage for future corporate leadership.* This management group, made up of the top twenty-five executives in the company, meets quarterly on companywide issues.

• *Top executives are encouraged to "broaden their portfolios,"* in McCaslin's words. "We like to keep challenging high-potential managers. We switch players around and give them the opportunity to succeed in different, key roles and gain new skills and experience."

• *While focusing on developing their own management, Continental Grain doesn't lose sight of what is happening on the outside:* "We benchmark key executives at regular intervals so we are always current in that market," says McCaslin.

As an important part of the process of evaluating potential CEO successors and the rest of the top management team, the board decided on the somewhat unusual step of having psychological evaluations done on all of these key people. Accordingly, a company that specializes in professional psychological evaluations of corporate management was brought in to do intensive interviewing of top executives at ContiGroup. The goal has been to understand individuals' strengths and weaknesses and to put them in the context of a larger picture: each individual executive's fit as a component of the top management team.

This new element in the process was launched four years ago, prior to Fribourg (the current CEO) being named president of Conti-Group. To gain a multidimensional picture of Fribourg and his personal and professional strengths and weaknesses, psychologists spent days interviewing him, his boss, the board, peers, and direct reports. After completing the interviews, the psychologists spent three days sharing their findings and conclusions with Fribourg and his wife.

Having survived the somewhat grueling, though thorough, process intact, Fribourg is a strong advocate of this approach. "Once you get to a certain level in a company, it's hard to get honest feedback. The process helped the company to identify areas we need to focus on and enlightened the board about individuals' capabilities short- and long-term." McCaslin, who has been through a somewhat truncated version of the same process, is similarly laudatory about its benefits to the company in terms of leadership planning. Both recommend the process to other companies to thoroughly evaluate the potential and fit of the top three to four senior managers.

Discussion of this holistic approach to surveying the top management team led Fribourg to comment on what he believes is a serious and common mistake companies make when hiring CEOs. "Often," Fribourg observed, "there is too much of a focus on the individual, rather than the team. It's essential to determine how well the personalities in the senior management team will fit together."

It was the board that made the decision that Fribourg should succeed Staheli. The transition took place over a two-year period, during which Fribourg was able to round out the skills and experience he would need to execute the CEO position. He took part in an outside training program at Harvard and began to take over gradual responsibility for those areas of the operation he had not previously been exposed to.

During the transition period, Fribourg worked closely with Staheli. The two looked long and hard at the management team and carefully assessed their resources: Who was effective and who was less effective? What gaps had to be filled because of retirement? "Based on his own experience, Don [Staheli] strongly recommended that we make whatever changes needed to be made in the management team as soon as possible. In retrospect, he felt that when he took over as CEO, he had not moved quickly enough," says Fribourg.

As ContiGroup has evolved from a grain company to an asset portfolio company, its leadership needs have necessitated a change from the traditional CEO to a financial services executive. An investment banker by training, Fribourg clearly fit the bill, but as a member of the founding family, he had to prove his mettle according to all objective criteria as much as if not more so than any family outsider.

When it comes to leadership development and succession issues, ContiGroup's systems and standards are as rigorous as any of the public companies we have studied. Fribourg sums up the approach: "The lesson for a private company is to run the business as professionally as you can . . . particularly if the CEO is an owner." With the help of his predecessor, an outstanding professional manager in anyone's book, Paul Fribourg has clearly earned the right to steer his family's company in a new direction.

Delta: Looking Beyond Today's Bottom Line

Formerly the preeminent U.S. airline and a leader in customer service, Delta Air Lines, Inc., had undergone some vast changes before they hired us to replace their longtime CEO, Ronald Allen. In response to poor financial performance from fiscal years 1991 through 1994, Allen had launched a major cost-cutting effort. The cost-cutting, combined with an improving economy and lower fuel prices, did lead to a resurgence in the company's financial performance. The company paid a high price internally for the improved financial health, however, and exacerbated a number of already existing problems which, if left unaddressed, could have a serious impact on future performance. As a result of the cutbacks:

- *Employee morale was at an all-time low.* Poor communications by senior management heightened the risk that Delta's nonunion (except for pilots) workforce would eventually be organized.

- *Customer service had deteriorated badly.* The once-great franchise had let its reputation as the leader in airline customer service slip away.

- *Bench strength was diminishing.* Cutbacks in staff had not allowed Delta to maintain the development of its management talent, and it was falling behind competitors in its ability to assemble a management team.

Delta's board became increasingly alarmed about the airline's overall health and future prospects and in the spring of '97 elected not to renew Allen's contract. The board had concluded that it could no longer accept what was occurring under Allen's stewardship and that he would have to be replaced.

Delta was perceived to be in a crisis mode. There was no highly respected CEO who would be retiring according to an orderly timetable; quite the contrary, the incumbent had been fired, and there would be an interim CEO during the search. Despite its still-strong balance sheet and large scale, Delta was in a precarious position. The absence of a strong executive at the helm combined with Delta's many assets and an industrywide consolidation made the company an attractive acquisition target for predators.

After the decision was made to find a replacement for Allen, we were brought in to implement a succession process with the board. The first step was to develop the position specification for the new CEO. To develop the spec, we met with the members of Delta's search committee, headed by Gerald Grinstein—former CEO of Burlington Northern Santa Fe Corp. and Western Airlines—and, interestingly, with leaders of employee groups. The board was very conscious of the need to improve communications around the company and wanted to solicit the views of the employee-group leaders.

The idea was not to put employees on the jury; the board recognized that deciding on a successor was ultimately its responsibility. Rather, this step was a signal that the Delta board cared about the opinions of long-service employees, who were viewed as essential to accomplishing Delta's strategic objectives. In fact, the insights culled from employee-group leaders were included in the list of key selection criteria drafted as a blueprint for the CEO search. Of particular note was the congruency between the views of the board and the heads of the employee organizations regarding the key elements in the ideal profile of Delta's new CEO.

The areas we explored with both groups to develop the spec included:

- their views of where the enterprise was heading and the *long-term goals;*

- *key selection criteria* they believed would be essential for the new CEO in order to develop and execute the strategy;

- in-depth exchange over *potential sources* of good candidates; particularly with the search committee, we explored those companies they respected and those known for breeding the skills we had identified in order to develop a target list of companies for potential candidates;

- *benchmarking individuals* known to both us and the search committee in potential target companies; where both we and the search committee were familiar with the same individuals, we tested the spec to get relevant benchmarks on how these individuals compared with our criteria.

After going through this initial process, we developed the spec that would guide us in our search for Delta's new CEO. Boiled down to its salient criteria, the individual we were seeking would have to:

- provide strategic leadership;

- have great people skills as well as proven communication skills;

- have strong customer service experience and the ability to balance investments in improved service with short-term financial performance;

- view the business globally.

When the short list of final candidates was considered by Delta's board, Leo Mullin emerged as their clear choice for Delta's new CEO. Mullin had demonstrated strong strategic ability as a young McKinsey partner and as head of strategy at Consolidated Rail Corp., as president and COO of First National Bank of Chicago, and as vice chairman at Unicom Corporation. He had built businesses, led turnarounds, and been steeped in the importance of customer service as he built the credit card and retail banking operations at First Chicago. He also possessed an international perspective and had demonstrated people skills. In short, he had all of the key criteria that had been set forth in the spec, and his ability and success in specific areas had been attested to by qualified references from his days at McKinsey, Conrail, First Chicago, and the giant midwestern utility Unicom.

The move to recruit Mullin was a bold and creative stroke by Delta's board to bring in an industry outsider. During careful and thoughtful deliberations, the board had determined that Mullin's eclectic experience, which encompassed strategy consulting, financial services, and customer service, was particularly well matched to the specific challenges Delta's new CEO would confront.

When Mullin was recruited to Delta in the early fall of 1997, the board made another thoughtful move: While appointing Mullin president and CEO, it also elected Grinstein nonexecutive chairman. This allowed Mullin to immediately focus on the company's strategic and operational challenges, while Grinstein focused on governance matters and various external constituencies. Grinstein made it clear that he would accept the position for a limited time, until it was clear that Delta was back on the right track.

The Delta case demonstrates how a board that was truly committed to following a rigorous and methodical succession process, and working as a team, was able to turn around a troubled company. We worked closely with them to develop a CEO spec that truly reflected the critical challenges the company was facing, then helped identify and recruit an individual who, while not necessarily the most obvious candidate, was clearly well suited by way of background, style, skills, and experience to tackle those challenges.

Mullin's finely honed strategic skills combined with his involvement in cutting-edge developments in retail financial services—with a focus on customer service—made him an ideal candidate for Delta's top spot. Moreover, this was the sort of turnaround situation that cried out for a fresh perspective. Given his expertise and point of view as an industry outsider, Mullin recognized that financial stability could not be achieved at the expense of employee morale and customer service.

In Mullin's first year as CEO the company had its first ever billion-dollar profit in a single fiscal year. And over the first twenty months of Mullin's tenure, Delta's share price has improved by more than 60 percent. Delta's solution was not just a quick fix, either; there are already longer-term and deeper-reaching benefits in terms of management development. As part of his mandate as CEO, Mullin has vowed to assemble a top-management team, effectively providing for his own succession, though that is not yet in the offing. To that end he has formed an executive management group that includes at least three potential long-term successors who not only work closely with him but also received extensive exposure to the board. Given the succession process now in place as a result of Mullin's and the board's efforts, it is likely that the next time Delta needs a CEO, it may need to look no further than its own backyard.

Board Checklist

What should boards do to oversee the creation and implementation of a process that will ensure smooth CEO succession and continual regeneration of corporate leadership? A few principles are worth focusing on:

1. The place for the board to start is by asking: Is there a clear process in place to ensure the availability of CEO candidates within the organization several years down the line? Does the board have the continual opportunity to monitor the process and to assess ongoing results?

2. The board must play a role in ensuring that the leadership development process is linked to the actual business strategy, by producing leaders who are capable of managing issues the company can expect to face. In a restructuring industry, for example, directors should ask themselves if a priority for a new CEO is experience in an industry or a company that has undergone similar shifts.

3. The board must assess the areas in which potential CEOs need additional training, and determine whether that is being provided by the CEO.

4. When hiring an outside consultant for assistance in succession, it is critical that the firm understand not only the personal criteria sought but also the strategic direction of the company and the link between the two.

5. In assessing the current CEO, boards must recognize the need to look beyond immediate profit/loss statements and get a sense of potential problems down the road—in communications, morale, or strategic shortsightedness—that may endanger the long-term financial future of the company.

What do the company examples discussed in this chapter and in other companies we have studied tell us about how boards should oversee the creation and implementation of a process that will ensure smooth CEO succession and continual regeneration of corporate leadership? We believe that whether a company is going through the more predictable routine of a retirement scenario with a highly respected CEO or is experiencing more turbulent times with a CEO who must be replaced in a rapidly changing industry, the best way to ensure that the most capable successor is ultimately selected is for the board to focus on a rational and reliable process. The added and very important benefit of implementing a process in which there are clearly identifiable, objective criteria is that it should give all contenders the satisfaction of knowing that they have a fair shot at the CEO spot. Moreover, the investment in process helps promote loyalty to the company by playing down the "horse race," and garners support for the successful candidate, making it possible for him or her to manage successfully.

More about laying the foundation for a reliable succession process —or what might more aptly be called a succession culture—as we take a closer look at the experiences of several best-practice companies in the next chapter, "Looking Deep Within the Organization."

4

Looking Deep Within the Organization

"I think that companies with succession/development cultures run better. It's not just about picking a new leader. The act of creating a mentality of development within a company makes for more effective operations even before the change takes place. People function better in a developmental mode. There's too much emphasis on the contingency aspect of succession—what happens if the CEO gets hit by a truck—and not enough on the development process. In my mind, it's about looking at someone on the succession ladder, evaluating his or her development needs, and doing something about them as early as possible."

—Frank Doyle, former executive vice president, General Electric

The most prevalent concept of succession planning still revolves around the notion of the CEO getting ready to step aside and pass the baton to a new CEO. The transition from one CEO to another is certainly a key element, and one of the most visible to outsiders, of the succession process, but it really is only the tip of the iceberg. Where do new leaders come from, and how can boards help to cultivate them? How can companies develop depth in leadership, not only a veneer at the top of the organization, but also horizontally, at every level, so that they need never worry about running out of talent? Important also is the ability to make successful transitions at the top without running the risk of losing substantial talent that companies may have spent years cultivating. These questions represent some of the complex issues we will deal with in this chapter as we once again draw on our experience with boards and CEOs, as well as specific cases of some best-practice companies, including those that have established some of the most successful and renowned training programs for world-class managers.

One thing is crystal clear to us from our own observations and feedback from directors and CEOs we work with: Companies that are truly successful at succession are those that focus not exclusively on the top of the organizational pyramid, but those that place just as much emphasis on building strength and leadership at every level. We like to use the term "succession culture" to describe this sort of planning because it conveys how integral it becomes, if done continuously and properly, to the fabric of the company. A fabric or matrix is, in fact, a good way of conceptualizing this culture—as opposed to the traditionally invoked leadership pipeline or hierarchy—because it describes the relationship and interdependency of the individuals at various levels who comprise the culture and suggests that the leadership development process is not strictly linear in nature.

The somewhat surprising truth is that there is still only a handful of companies (perhaps, at the most, eight to ten worldwide) that are truly successful at developing cadres of good general managers—that is, the sorts of executives who can ultimately be groomed to take on the responsibilities of a CEO. We use the word "surprising" because while companies have devised all sorts of sophisticated, scientific techniques and made quantum leaps in certain areas in recent years—whether in technology, in creating sophisticated alliances, in marketing, or in financial engineering—when it comes to developing leaders, it is the same few companies that everyone points to. Why is it that when the subject is developing management talent, that the first examples that come to mind on a very short list always include General Electric, Pepsi, Motorola, Emerson Electric, and very few others? What are these companies doing that others are not, and what can we learn from them?

The answer is that while many companies make it a priority to hire the right CEO, few recognize the importance of shaping an ongoing process that will train and retain talented managers today, excellent executives tomorrow, and the potential CEO who can provide leadership in the future. Those that do focus on the ongoing process do it consistently, in both good and less-good times. Even when these leaders may be experiencing problems in the marketplace, they continue to place great emphasis on management development and the succession process.

One indicator of how unsuccessful most companies have been at developing their own management talent is the degree to which our business has been thriving. Are we worried about sowing the seeds of our own obsolescence by telling companies how they can develop a system of self-renewing leadership from the bottom up? Not at all. We believe that many companies rely too heavily on executive search to compensate for their inability to grow their own leaders. We would go even further and say that, based on our experience, there is clearly something dysfunctional in a company that has not developed capable replacement leadership, particularly at the very top. Often it relates to the unwillingness or inability of the CEO to anoint an insider as successor or, if no suitable inside successor exits, to take action to find one outside the organization.

This leads us back to an important premise for this book, and one we have reinforced at every appropriate opportunity: The management development/succession agenda must be driven by the board. These processes are too vital to the health and continued existence of the organization to be left solely in the hands of the CEO, who may be unable or unwilling, or who, even with the best intentions, may procrastinate when it comes to pushing leadership development forward.

Identifying and Nurturing Talent

Why do so many companies fail to achieve a succession culture? Perhaps because so many immediate issues that have visible impact on revenue, costs, and share value prevent succession from reaching the top of the agenda. That is one of the conclusions reached by Stephen Sass after decades of dealing with leadership development issues as president of a performance consulting firm, director in charge of the Center for Leadership Development for KPMG Peat Marwick, LLP, and twenty-eight years with IBM in customer service and education executive management.

According to Sass, one must first establish a culture that is conducive to developing management talent. "Succession planning and people management stuff in general are usually low urgency, high importance. In other words, it's important, but no one's breathing down your neck to get it done. The board has to heighten the sense of urgency so that these things will get the attention they deserve and the organization will get the real payoff that comes from addressing people management thoughtfully. So if you have an organization that recognizes the importance of these responsibilities and a board that is willing to put the structure behind it—quarterly management reviews, annual reviews, regular discussion of CEO successors— that's how it gets accomplished."

One of the most important elements in developing leadership potential is identifying the people who have it, in order to focus on shaping a path for them to progress through the organization. Sass comments, "Think of a typical organization as a series of four concentric circles: The outermost circle consists of the general population; the second, people in first-line leadership positions; the third, middle management; the fourth, top management—division presidents, vice presidents, directors, people at the policy level. You need a process that recognizes that these circles exist—that they expand and contract—and that you must go from one to the next. The process is called something different in different organizations; it might be called succession, executive continuity, early ID, but it has the same basic elements. It's a way of identifying people with the talent and interest in succeeding in a company and then creating a system that helps them develop their skills and work through the circles, from one level to the next."

Identifying what is often referred to as "high potential" talent at an early stage and bringing it along through each of these levels or circles represent a huge commitment and investment by the corporation. Perhaps this helps to explain why so few companies do it well. But in contrast to the "organization man" days of the 1950s, people are far more mobile and less inclined to remain with a company unless it allows them to develop and grow and unless it rewards them for their contribution.

An important part of the development process consists of current leaders formally and informally acknowledging those who have been singled out as important to the future of the organization. Ideally this is done early in one's development in an organization and reinforced regularly. Many companies and professional firms, for example, have orientation programs that are intended to expose up-and-coming executives to leaders of the firm and to send a message that the organization values them.

Recognition in a less formal way—the general out among the troops—also can be a very powerful way of sending the message "We value your contribution and you're destined for great things if you build a career with us." Sass relates the story of a friend who was visiting with former Netscape Communications Corp. CEO James Barksdale (now managing partner of The Barksdale Group) over lunch in the company's cafeteria. As they were leaving the cafeteria, Barksdale put his arm around a scruffy kid and turned to the other executive, saying, "I want you to meet Mike. He's been here for three months and he's doing the most fantastic things for us!" The influence of the CEO on the development of future leaders, merely by virtue of his personal interest, should not be underestimated.

The relationship between the organization and the developing executive needs to be further cemented and recognized each time he or she moves to a new level. "There should be a watershed event—call it charm school for executives—where you are initiated into the next level. When I was first made a manager at IBM, I received six books that spelled out Tom Watson's philosophy. Once you became a manager, you had to go to new manager's school within thirty days." This was how IBM demonstrated its commitment to the success of developing future leaders, and to ensuring future success as a company by continually nurturing its freshest talent.

Companies that are serious about developing leaders won't let their commitment wane; the effort and investment of the company are likely to increase as the executive makes his or her way up the ladder. At each level—general employee population to first-line manager to middle manager, etc.—company and employee go through the same two-step process. The employer wants to know, "Do you have what it takes to go further?" and "What can we do to develop your potential?" Once you're developing those who will go beyond first-line managers, you need to consider a structured program with tried-and-true elements that many of the best companies use to their advantage when nurturing leadership talent. These include elements such as 360-degree feedback, where a range of supervisors, colleagues, and reports provides confidential information on one's strengths and weaknesses as a manager; participation in task forces; and establishing a set of desirable "competencies," as well as a process that identifies gaps in skills and a process to close them.

There are a couple of elements critical to making the development process work, particularly when you get to the executive ranks:

- Aspiring leaders must have exposure to the board so that directors can get to know them and help monitor their development.

- People must be given meaningful assignments so that they can really develop their potential.

Sass puts direct emphasis on the word "meaningful." "This is where people have the greatest opportunity to grow the most," he says, "but they need real assignments, real work, not theoretical exercises. People want to be coached and guided to minimize mistakes and failure, but they also want to make an impact—in business assignments, in client situations, on task forces."

Develop a Leadership Profile and Stretch Talent

According to Richard Randazzo—senior vice president of human resources at Federal-Mogul Corporation and formerly vice president, personnel, U.S. Marketing Group at Xerox Corporation—those companies, Xerox among them, renowned for developing great leaders and consistent bench strength start early. "IBM, Xerox, Procter & Gamble, 3M, Hewlett-Packard, and others like them—these are companies that have a prescribed hiring profile right off the college campus. I think you would find that GE does an immense amount of hiring at the lower levels within their organization, and there is a profile. Xerox, without a doubt, has a prescribed profile. There's nothing in writing, but it's been going on for so long that everyone is familiar with it. It was started by a small nucleus of people, and it just perpetuates itself. I hire people who look like me, who think like me, who act like me, who share my values, in terms of results, orientation, aggressiveness, and even appearance. You can walk into a restaurant and you can say, 'You work for IBM or Xerox, don't you,' and you'll get a 'Yes.' You can pick them out."

Once you identify and recruit good people, if you really want to develop talent and keep it coming from the bottom up, Randazzo says, the other thing that seems to happen fairly early is that you give these people a lot of responsibility early on, responsibility that stretches their ability and is not highly structured, so people have to make their own decisions and live with the consequences. "Welch at GE just did this last year, and it was very well publicized. He basically said, 'Everybody stand up and rotate chairs.' So he had people who are in his nuclear power plant business running lightbulbs, and the lightbulb guys are in charge of turbines. So you stretch talent. It allows people to test their management capabilities and puts them in an unfamiliar environment. You want to test whether someone is success-oriented or has a high success quotient, so you put the people in crisis situations.

"What you see emerging are people who can handle challenges; they may be given responsibilities no one has ever been given before, or somebody else may have screwed it up royally, and you get to go in and fix it.... What starts to happen is that the successful people start moving up the organization." Those who are not successful are weeded out, and those who are successful but do not ultimately get the top leadership position leave for other opportunities."

"That's why," Randazzo says, "you constantly have to feed the system at the bottom. In order to get good people, you have to come to terms with the fact that, even though you may not like it, you also become a developer of talent for others. It just happens. If you have the talent, and it shows itself, others will come seek that kind of talent from you."

GE: Master of Leadership Development

Few companies demonstrate Randazzo's point as well as General Electric. Perhaps the best proof of GE's ability to groom top managers is not even found at GE, but at all of the other companies that are run by CEOs that GE trained: Goodyear Tire & Rubber Co., which hired former GEer Stanley Gault as its CEO; AlliedSignal, Inc., which hired away Lawrence Bossidy; or Amgen, whose COO, Kevin Sharer, was a top manager at GE.

Almost invariably, General Electric is at the top of the list when people are talking about companies that have consistently been able to develop world-class leadership. What does GE do to constantly develop and reinforce a succession culture that is the envy of many other companies, a culture that has not only developed a bench of outstanding leaders for itself but that also has helped to populate the CEO offices of many other leading companies?

Frank Doyle, who, when he retired from GE in 1995, was executive vice president and a member of the three-person executive office (which, of course, included CEO John "Jack" Welch), provides some insights. Interestingly, the executive office was not intended as a succession vehicle, but more to provide a peer group with which the CEO could work, to keep his workload "rational," and to assist the business heads in doing their jobs. Doyle's comments provide a glimpse inside the much-admired and apparently hard-to-replicate leadership development process at GE.

According to Doyle, GE does development and succession "wall to wall," starting at the most elemental root level all the way up to the top, and it is always a clear priority. GE has had a long-standing commitment, for example, to recruit off college campuses, in good times and in bad—even during periods of dramatic reductions in the total workforce. From the moment these new recruits join the company, they enter a developmental culture, where they take part in annual reviews and are frequently in and out of educational programs and GE's Management Development Institute. Meaningful, hands-on assignments—as suggested earlier—to round out the experience and skills of up-and-coming executives are an important part of management development at GE.

All of the top people at GE, from the CEO on down, are involved in the education process, sending a strong signal about its value to the company. "Jack Welch interacts with managers in the company to an extraordinary degree, and he invests a lot of time and effort in getting to know people. He is as rigorous in pursuing people resources as he is business issues. I almost have a feeling of disbelief when I hear myself say that now, but it's true—he devotes as much time to people as anything else," says Doyle.

Welch, William Conaty, GE's senior vice president of human resources, and other senior management regularly review management resources on location at various GE businesses, where they will typically spend two days and review two layers of direct reports below the CEO level. Welch and his top-management team gain plenty of exposure to those making their way up the ranks, and Welch is famous among CEOs for knowing literally thousands of the people who work for GE and for maintaining personal contact, including handwritten, heartfelt personal notes to more than a few.

In addition, Welch and other top managers regularly put themselves on the line by "working the pit," as Doyle and other GEers refer to it: lecturing and then responding to challenges from "students," high-potential managers at "Crotonville," the Croton-on-Hudson campus where the company runs its management-development programs.

The constant nurturing of management talent, in both formal and informal ways, is part of the secret of GE's success, and it is by now an integral part of the culture for which the company has become known. "The science is good," says Doyle, "but the dedication and involvement are even more impressive." And future leaders clearly thrive in this environment. "People know that when Welch and Company come into town they're going to spend time, ask a lot of questions. People get direct personal feedback; they know it's an evaluation culture, that they're being watched and invested in."

The message that education and development are among the

CEO's highest priorities filters down to everyone else in the organization. "If someone is selected for a leadership development course at Crotonville, a business leader would be at peril if he made an excuse that the executive could not be spared," states Doyle.

As Welch, GE's charismatic and revered CEO, approaches retirement age, there is increasing speculation about "life after Jack," and the likelihood of naming a leader of the same caliber to replace him. According to Doyle, GE insiders are notably unconcerned. "They've been through all that before," he observes. "The same questions were posed when Reg Jones (Welch's predecessor) retired. He was such an important industrial leader and people were looking at Jack and saying, 'Who is this young guy from plastics?' During the time of the transition, 1981, *Fortune* magazine ran an article on GE as the best-run company in America with the most-respected executive group and the best farm team for all the other companies in the industry." Clearly Welch was subject to the same speculation about being able to fill his predecessor's shoes as his successor will be when the time comes for Welch to step down.

While much is also made by those who observe the company of the horse-race culture, Doyle does not believe that insiders experience it as such. He believes that the twelve business heads relate to one another in a free-flowing, boundariless way and that any sort of negative competition to move one ahead is something that Welch and others simply would not tolerate. "Those sorts of tactics would get you knocked off the succession ladder faster than anything I know." The emphasis is on working as part of a team, and "if feeling indispensable is part of your psyche, you'd better go somewhere else."

GE apparently works on succession in a very orderly, systematic way, maintaining a timeline that plots when key people in the organization will leave. Below that top level, there is a wide array of people who are considered legitimate contenders for the top job who are evaluated according to their level of mastery in a number of critical areas—including whether they have acquired sufficient experience in an international business and in running an independent business— that anyone who would be seriously considered for the CEO's job would have to possess.

"We would make sure they were getting the right exposure and that the pool was big enough. If you want to avoid the horse race, it's best to keep the field as big as possible." The field of contenders would comprise close to two dozen of the most promising executives, any of whom, Doyle insists, could run a good-size company. Could and do, based on GE's track record of providing CEOs for other top companies. In fact, Doyle points out, of the original group of nine who comprised Reginald "Reg" Jones's (Welch's predecessor) top team, six ended up highly successful CEOs. GE has provided a wealth of talented executives, not only for itself but, perhaps more than any company in existence, for other companies as well.

Does GE itself ever go outside to fill important management spots? Rarely for operating management, though occasionally for specific staff positions. Because it is one of the few remaining highly successful, huge conglomerates, when GE needs an individual with particular outside or cross-industry experience, more than likely, someone meeting the requirements may be found in one of GE's many diverse businesses. These businesses may not cultivate the expertise needed for specific staff positions, such as general counsel, which might necessitate an outside recruitment. As part of the leadership development process, however, Doyle says, the company does maintain an awareness of what other companies are doing.

Whether talk is about the management development process, CEO selection process, or anything else at GE, the conversation inevitably begins and ends with Jack Welch. In fact, few companies are identified so closely with their CEO. One should not make the mistake of assuming, however, that Welch single-handedly runs the show. In fact, he works in close partnership with the board's management development and compensation committee headed by Silas Cathcart, former CEO of Illinois Tool Works. According to *Corporate Board Member*, "That same group of five keeps GE's top 130 executives under constant scrutiny. New managerial assignments are handed down with an eye toward assessing future CEO material. In addition, the committee formally evaluates GE's top 15 executives at six-monthly intervals by talking to peers, subordinates, managers, and even retired executives for a more objective read."

When it comes down to it, the development process at GE is bigger than any one executive—even Jack Welch—and so good that even if top talent is occasionally picked off by competitors, more talent is continually coming up, making more than enough to go around.

SmithKline Beecham: A Postmerger Commitment to Development

Six weeks into his tenure as CEO in April 1994, Jan Leschly, CEO of SmithKline Beecham, was already planning for his successor. In a meeting at SmithKline Beecham's Philadelphia offices, Daniel Phelan, senior vice president and director of human resources, detailed the development of a structure for succession planning with the board. Prior to the merger of SmithKline Beckman Corp. and Beecham Group PLC in July 1989, neither company had a history of success in developing future leaders. After the merger, former SmithKline chairman and CEO Henry Wendt, and former Beecham chairman Robert Bauman made the identification of SmithKline Beecham's next chief executive a top priority. The result of this concerted effort was the recruitment of the current CEO, Jan Leschly, and COO Jean-Pierre Garnier.

According to the pattern now established, Phelan reviews with the board the Leadership Planning Process, which includes the development process for some forty-five hundred employees in middle-management positions through those in the senior management ranks. Leschly makes a presentation to the board—a sort of "state of the union" message—that includes an EEO profile on the number and development of women and minorities, an update on the pipeline at the director level, five-year goals, and an evaluation of his top-management team.

In addition, Leschly and his team devote two days annually to taking a complete inventory of SmithKline Beecham's talent. According to Phelan, the process has been developed with line executives and the emphasis is on "How can we improve the business?" And though facilitated by the human resources function, it is "not a human resources thing." A similar review is conducted in all the businesses at the area and country levels and in the staff functions.

The inventory is only one element of the process. Once talent in the organization is identified, there is a major emphasis on exposing that talent to the right conditions so that high-potential executives will grow into leaders for the company. Since Phelan believes that most development is a result of exposure to different job experiences, that means moving promising candidates through a series of carefully selected, increasingly responsible positions.

SmithKline Beecham demonstrates a strong commitment to growing people internally, and Phelan says they believe that the top-person must understand all three of the company's businesses. "We ideally follow a '2+2+2' formula in developing people for top-management positions," explains Phelan, which translates as building a track record with experience in two business units, two functional areas, and two countries. The process is not only intended to continue to supply the organization with leaders, it also helps individuals in the company acquire the skills and experience they will need to build successful careers. "The earlier in someone's career we are able to plan, the more we are able to ensure that they won't end up in the heap."

SmithKline Beecham's commitment to developing its own talent grows out of some hard-learned lessons. Before the merger, according to Phelan, both companies were very much inbred and rarely went outside to fill senior positions. As a result, the new company did extensive outside recruiting to fill top positions after the merger. "It was demoralizing to many people," says Phelan.

Even with a well-established development plan now in place, the company continues to look externally to fill positions at the director level and above some 20 to 30 percent of the time to add fresh ideas and approaches to the existing mix, which helps to stimulate the organization. "The ideal is that you want to grow internally, but the fact is that there's never enough talent," concludes Phelan. In an effort to attract the person best suited for each position, the question of inside vs. outside recruitment is carefully considered by the hiring

executive every time there is a vacancy in the top three hundred positions in the company.

GTE's Directors: An Integral Part of the Development Process

How can a company ensure that outside directors are given an inside
view of the company and its management team? GTE Corporation
has made it a priority, and has shaped a process that gives directors a
long view of the company's succession potential and the opportunity
to provide feedback. Director involvement has become an
entrenched tradition at GTE, and it is one that appears likely to live
on after the merger with Bell Atlantic, given that company's similar
emphasis on leadership development, succession, and strong independent directors.

At GTE, board involvement has been recognized as a crucial aspect
of leadership development since 1981. To facilitate the board's role,
the company has institutionalized a highly structured and formalized
CEO succession/leadership development process. At the core of the
process is the review of key managers, an annual exercise with the
board. Directors are given the tools to determine how well leaders are
actually being developed, and to assess future potential corporate
leadership.

Succession planning is part of an annual cycle that renews itself
each spring, prior to the March board meeting. At that time, a bot-
tom-up evaluation (with those in each level assessing their direct
reports) of GTE's management is initiated, starting with those at the
broad base of the management pyramid and ascending to the tip of
the pyramid, the office of the chairman.

For those nearing the upper leadership ranks in the company—the
top thirty executives—a detailed evaluation is prepared and included
in a book for directors, which gives a snapshot of each executive's
performance, accomplishments, and anticipated future potential to
the company. This last slot will indicate future assignments or development opportunities two to three years and three to five years into
the future. In some cases the category that describes these suggested

grooming opportunities is left blank, indicating that this individual reports to a member of the office of the chairman, and that he or she is perceived to have "unlimited potential"—that is, that he or she might be a possible future contender for the chairman's job.

The board evaluates those at the top of the organization—the chairman, president, and vice chairman—who together comprise the office of the chairman. The office of the chairman serves two complementary functions at GTE. First, it serves to redistribute power at the top of the company among a group of the seniormost executives. Further, it provides a variety of learning experiences for the most likely successors for the chairman's job, and it provides an opportunity for the chairman and the board to assess their performance and their suitability to run the company.

During the March board meeting, each member of the office of the chairman presents evaluations of his own reports to the board. These top fifteen up-and-comers—the "leadership committee"—are well known to directors, who are continually kept apprised of assignments they are being given to round out their development as the leaders they will be in the not-too-distant future. Exposure of these executives and the opportunity for directors and the chairman to observe them in a variety of contexts are assured, not only through periodic board meetings but also at two annual functions—the year-end celebration, and an off-site three-day meeting with the board—as well as other occasions, such as retirement parties for board members.

Those a bit further down the line as far as succession—whom J. Randall MacDonald, GTE's executive vice president for human resources and administration refers to as "long-runway people"— also have ample opportunity to develop leadership skills and to demonstrate that they have the right stuff. This next generation of leaders, the thirty- to thirty-nine-year-olds, are given frequent opportunities to hone their management skills as members of task forces and in presentations to the board. "The exposure of senior management and the next level down to the board is all part of the socialization process," says MacDonald. "We're conscious of the importance of giving directors the opportunity to get to know these people and to see them in action. It's a key element in the succession process."

Bestfoods: Cross-training Ground

The CEO has to be knowledgeable about all areas of a company's performance and familiar with each of its units. How does a company ensure that promising executives obtain the breadth of experience they will need to take over the leadership of the company? Bestfoods' CEO and board continually focus on this goal and make every effort to instill a companywide view and correspondingly broad-based skills in its executives well before they reach the top ranks.

"Ideally we would like to cross-train early, before people become solidly entrenched in their careers," says CEO Charles Shoemate. "Divisions that are able to do that best also produce the best management talent."

But at any given time, succession planning is a balancing act, particularly between what are perceived as the needs of the business and the needs of a particular candidate. Ensuring that managers at Bestfoods acquire multiple experiences early on is not always an easy task. As Shoemate explains, Bestfoods is in a consumer business, and marketing is the function of choice. "It's hard to get marketing people to move out of marketing."

In spite of the difficulties, Bestfoods continues to take on the challenge of broadening the perspective of company leaders. In addition to cross-training in a variety of functions, Bestfoods uses its strategy committee to encourage its senior executives to consider the impact of decisions on the company as a whole and not just on their area. From five to seven of Bestfoods' seniormost executives serve on the committee, including top candidates in line to succeed the CEO. Aside from formal meetings four times a year for one and a half days at a time, this group spends several hours a month in phone meetings, a week on division strategies, and the yearly collaborative effort to put together the book on the one hundred senior managers for the board.

And the board plays an active role, obtaining a clear sense of how well leaders at all levels are progressing, with a close eye on the breadth of experience they are acquiring. "The board is continually assessing with me the progress of various managers," says Shoemate. "In our executive sessions they'll ask, 'How's Joe doing? How's Sue doing? How's such-and-such a rotation progressing?'" Directors find it easy to track the career of up-and-comers because, like other best-practice companies, Bestfoods has a system in place to continually expose leading succession candidates to the board. According to human resources senior vice president Richard Bergeman, each of the company's twenty to thirty top managers "gets as much face time with the board as possible each year," including formal presentations and one-on-one lunches with directors.

For Bestfoods, such methods as cross-training, varied job experience, and direct board involvement help to create potential leaders with a full grasp of the company's operations.

Warner-Lambert: Signal from the Top

Four times a year the former CEO of Warner-Lambert Company, Melvin Goodes—who stepped down in May 1999 and was succeeded by Lodewijk J. R. de Vink, previously president and COO—would hold one-on-one meetings with three junior executives of his firm, all in their thirties. At these quarterly meetings the young executives got a chance to discuss issues related to their careers and to discuss any problems or questions they may have had concerning their future in the company. The process, commonly known as mentoring, was something Goodes simply considered part of his job. Through his own actions Goodes broadcasted the importance of developing, rewarding, and retaining talent. What had long been a priority of the CEO became a priority for the entire organization. But the message was clearly generated from the top.

Goodes understood the impact of the CEO's behavior on retaining valuable employees. "Part of my job," he says plainly, "was to keep people happy. I was with big companies for forty years and only one person reporting to me left voluntarily. I'm proud of that."

Goodes' commitment is reflected in a process called "talent planning." Every year the CEO reviews succession planning—including immediate contingency plans should anything happen to him—and deeper-level management reviews with the board. In addition, once a year the CEO goes off-site with the six members of the office of the chairman, where they devote three days to talent planning, reviewing the development of some two hundred to three hundred managers. Who are their potential replacements? What course should their training take in the immediate and longer-term future? CEO and crew focus on identifying those at the highest levels who will eventually replace the twenty members of Warner-Lambert's management committee.

Management development experts invariably emphasize the importance of identifying, molding, and nurturing talent at an early stage, and Warner-Lambert evidently excels at this. In a business such as Warner-Lambert's, which encompasses all global markets, talent that is skilled at cross-border transactions is especially vital. Helping younger managers plan careers and develop required skills early on is particularly crucial to the company's success.

"Historically there have been problems—with us and other global companies—getting people to move internationally," says Goodes. "That's why it's so important to work with people and help them develop their career before they have family responsibilities, before they have kids in school—while they still have the flexibility to move around." To help build a corps of capable international executives, the company identifies promising individuals just emerging from graduate school and targets them for a special program in which they are groomed for international assignments.

One of the best examples of Goodes' personal commitment is the mentoring program. Originally it just involved the office of the chairman. Focused on supporting diversity—which included assisting in the development of women and minorities—it was a way of sending a message straight from the top. What began as a limited initiative among the company's top six officers has spread in ripples to the farthest reaches of the company's management. "There are a hundred people in the mentoring program now," Goodes says proudly, "and it reaches down to the sales districts." While the office of the chairman created the mentoring program, its movement deeper and deeper into the organization was powered by word of mouth and individual initiative.

In addition to women and minorities, the mentoring initiative is targeted at employees in remote operations, including overseas, who might not automatically be on the radar screen of those assessing upcoming talent. The mission is to identify high-potential managers, wherever they may be, and expose them to the company's senior executives. "We try to group people from different parts of the company so that they are exposed to different points of view and get more objective advice," explains Goodes.

Pride and personal satisfaction in the mentoring program are readily evident when Goodes talks about his own involvement. "I've seen my first-year mentees go on to bigger and better things in the company and I feel really good about that." Goodes obviously found the coaching, people-development aspect of the job most gratifying and, equally important, he made an ongoing "mission statement" about the company: that Warner-Lambert greatly values the leadership identification and development process and that everyone in the company, from the CEO on down, must commit the time and effort to making sure it succeeds.

The Costs and Benefits of Developing Talent

Though not every company is a GE, a PepsiCo, or an IBM when it comes to a track record of developing leadership systematically throughout the company, just about everyone admires this approach and agrees that homegrown talent is a highly desirable goal. Except under extraordinary circumstances—for example, rapidly changing conditions in the industry and a lack of leaders adequately prepared to deal with these conditions, or a new set of skills needed that have not been anticipated by development programs—there is much to be said for an inwardly focused development and recruitment process, including:

• an increased pool of talent and shortened leadership gaps;

- less risk in appointment decisions as a result of "seeing candidates in action";

- possibly less costly than using external candidates, especially when hidden benefits are factored in (e.g., possibly improved employee morale and productivity from continuity and stability, and possibly improved customer satisfaction and loyalty);

- potential for more stable, even improved, market capitalization because of confidence in leadership continuity and direction.

With all of the obvious benefits of leadership development and internally rather than externally focused recruitment efforts, why doesn't every company go this route? The answer is a simple one: time and money. Though the advantages are clear, a truly well-designed and well-implemented top-to-bottom leadership development program requires a tremendous investment of time and money. That means a commitment from all, including current leaders who may pay lip service to the importance of nurturing talent but whose real priorities may lie elsewhere.

There are significant costs for the corporation that undertakes leadership development in a serious and comprehensive way. Major direct cost categories of investing in this approach include:

- recruiting and selection staff and expense;

- orientation and assimilation of new employees;

- development and maintenance of competencies;

- implementation of a leadership selection and development process: leadership potential identification and selection, programs to teach basics at each milestone, advanced and renewal programs, cost of internal and external faculty, costs of staff coordination and oversight;

- senior leadership involvement.

Clearly we believe the benefits add up. As former Harvard University president Derek Bok once said, "Anyone concerned about the cost of education should consider the cost of ignorance." Similarly, companies scared off by the cost of leadership development should consider the potential cost of a leadership vacuum.

Holding On to Talent You've Developed

Companies that invest in their people must take an increasingly important factor into consideration: the more valuable an executive becomes to the company, the more valuable he or she will likely be to competitors. Ironically, the better job a company does at developing a world-class cadre of executives, the greater the risk of losing them. There is tremendous demand among our clients for executives who have been trained at Pepsi and other "academy" companies. Candidly, that is one of the reasons why we don't work for them; they are a tremendous resource for our other clients.

How can companies—especially those renowned for developing the best leadership—guard against losing valuable leaders? What sort of preemptive moves can they make to hold on to talented executives who represent the future of their company? There are a number of creative ways in which companies can reward and effectively retain executive talent, and they fall into three general categories:

- *financial incentives* that have been aided and improved by a strong stock market; we'll explore this category further in chapter 7, which deals with financial tools that promote succession planning;

- *psychological incentives*, with which companies can increase the personal job satisfaction of top managers;

- *organizational incentives*, wherein companies make actual structural changes allowing top executives the greatest latitude in exercising their leadership skills, effectively giving them authority over their own "company."

The importance of psychological rewards that satisfy the ego of the seniormost executives and encourage them to remain with a company should not be underestimated. We've observed a change in the titles that designate top corporate executives in recent years—from general manager to president, for example. This trend has partly been spurred by the decentralization of many companies and a move away from the headquarters concept and toward the concept that large corporations are federations of individual businesses. Not only are there great psychological rewards for managers who are able to run their own show, but also companies often find that such arrangements provide great returns for them. Larger companies have discovered that by finding ways to inject some entrepreneurial vigor—previously more characteristic of smaller ventures—and allowing managing executives greater control over their destiny and that of the company, they can produce impressive results for both the individual and the company.

A number of companies have taken this entrepreneurial approach a step further by changing the fundamental structure of these subsidiaries and making them, for all intents and purposes, completely separate companies. We referred to this relatively new phenomenon, known as the "equity carve-out," as "a new spin on the corporate structure" in an article we coauthored with McKinsey and Blue Capital Investment for a 1997 issue of *The McKinsey Quarterly*.

An equity carve-out is the sale by a public company of a portion of one of its subsidiaries' common stocks through an initial public offering (IPO). Each carved-out subsidiary has its own board, operating CEO, and financial statements, while the parent provides strategic direction and central resources. As in any other corporate structure, the parent can provide executive management skills, industry and government relations, and employee plans, and perform time-consuming administrative functions, freeing the subsidiary's CEO to concentrate on products and markets.

For *The McKinsey Quarterly* we examined the performance of U.S. equity carve-out subsidiaries from 1985 to 1995, in cases where 50 percent or more of each subsidiary's shares were retained by the parent. The results suggested that equity carve-outs are an effective way for companies to exploit growth opportunities and increase shareholder value.

The human resources benefits also were striking. In carve-outs, corporate boards can use the market to align pay closely with performance—ordinarily a tricky formula to achieve in a larger corporate setting—by awarding managers stock in their own carved-out units rather then cash bonuses and/or parent company stock. The payback is clear: increased entrepreneurialism, which benefits the parent company, the subsidiary, and top managers alike. As the CEO of one carve-out put it, "What you do is represented in the stock price."

Money is not the only incentive, however. The carve-out structure also responds to the psychological needs of high-performing executives to be autonomous. Business unit presidents are no longer bit players in a billion-dollar company; they are CEOs. This psychological satisfaction has an important effect on top-leadership talent when they are deciding whether to remain with a company or, alternatively, to seek another position where they can have a greater impact and reap more personal rewards.

We have been able to quantify this long-held belief by examining data from a number of our recent CEO assignments. Of forty-one CEO assignments over an eight-month period, 65 percent were filled by executives who were number two in their previous companies and who were motivated by the desire to run an independent operation. We'll explore factors and strategies specifically related to retaining these number twos in chapter 6, which focuses on those next in line to the CEO.

In addition to the benefits of improving executive and company performance and providing for the psychological needs of highly valued executives, subsidiary carve-outs serve as breeding grounds for candidates who might succeed senior executives in the parent company. Here, subsidiary CEOs get the chance to prove their business acumen and ability to work with their own board of directors. In discussions with GTE, SmithKline Beecham, and other best practice companies, we have learned that they consider board experience an important criterion when considering internal candidates for succession.

Board Practices That Promote a Succession Culture

We close with answers to a question we posed at the beginning of the chapter, regarding what sort of board involvement is appropriate in developing leadership within a company. Independent directors are, after all, by definition outsiders, and while they are charged with the responsibility of overseeing management activities, they should not be involved in actively managing the company.

In a company that has developed a true succession culture, the board will have regular exposure to—and thus ample opportunity to interact with and evaluate—the top-leadership team, including senior staff and those heading business units. Frequent and direct exposure to this group is crucial to effective succession planning, because this is the group from which any inside successor to the CEO will likely be drawn, and the board needs plenty of opportunity to see individuals in action, in a variety of roles, and taking on a variety of challenges in order to assess their personal style and skills.

Those who comprise the top-management team should be regularly exposed to the board in a variety of ways: as resources to board committees; presenting strategic studies and business plans to the board; presenting market or opportunity analyses; and involved in regulatory and key customer issues. Periodic social occasions with the board—dinners, lunches after board meetings—provide important opportunities for directors to assess the softer, personal characteristics of potential successors, which can be as important in the top-leadership role as the more concrete, easier-to-evaluate, business skills and experience.

This group of senior officers is generally considered above the level at which executive development programs are deemed appropriate. This does not mean that they have nothing more to learn, only that they are likely at this stage to get their continued "education" as they grapple with the challenges of the day-to-day business. The CEO, in discussion with the board, may decide to rotate various individuals in a new business sector or staff position to test them in a new role and to complete their seasoning as a potential successor. These sorts of decisions are often made in sessions between the CEO and the board as they review the progress of leading candidates to succeed the CEO.

Companies with succession cultures engage in this exercise at least once or twice a year, and perhaps as often as every board meeting if the CEO is close to retiring. The result is that the board is intimately familiar with key players who are in the running to be CEO. More than names or photos in a glossy presentation book, they are real, three-dimensional human beings whose efforts and results they have been able to observe and evaluate firsthand. Though directors will obviously not have been able to observe potential successors in every possible situation, they should know individuals well enough to be able to predict how well they might perform under a wide range of conditions as CEO.

Below the level of senior officers, the board is generally less intimately familiar with a company's managers. Not only would it be impractical for independent directors to be involved in executive development efforts, it also would conflict with what is normally viewed as the board's role—as overseer of management. As we have explored somewhat in other chapters, some boards do become directly involved with operations—dropping in on businesses while traveling, even "adopting" executives and serving as mentors—but most companies do not countenance this sort of direct involvement in managing the company. This sort of interaction is widely viewed, and we agree, as usurping the role of the company's senior line management.

A key underlying assumption, as we have discussed the various elements of developing and maintaining a succession culture, is that nurturing leadership and grooming internal successors is the preferred route to take. And we should state, once again for the record, that we definitely advocate this approach. We are frequently called in when, for one reason or another, companies have failed to develop their own successors or have found the internal path impossible or impractical. Over the long term, however, the most successful companies have strong succession cultures, even if they occasionally are forced to go outside to recruit talent.

As we have seen, those companies with true succession cultures are among the most successful, most envied, and most raided in corpo-

rate America. When companies produce their own internal successors they reinforce the cohesiveness of the organization and maxi-
mize employee morale and productivity. They also reinforce continuity and stability with key constituencies, including clients/
customers, investors, suppliers, industry groups, and regulators or
government groups.

Of course, there is not always an appropriate internal candidate, as
we well know from our own work. Often companies have failed to
develop the necessary bench strength, and no one is prepared to succeed to a top position. Alternatively, the incumbent may have been a
poor performer, and any logical successors may be ill prepared to
take over or tainted by their association with the unsuccessful executive. A significant change in strategic direction may also necessitate
the recruitment of outside leaders if no one internally is qualified to
take on the new challenges. New leadership may also result from
merger and acquisition activity, where one company's management
gains dominance over another.

Board Checklist

There are proven steps that companies can take to develop a succession culture. In our board checklist for chapter 4 we recommend
what we view as necessary and appropriate board involvement at
each stage of the development and succession process:

1. Board ensures that succession/management development is
    a matter of high priority for both the board and CEO by:

    • devoting at least two board meetings a year (more if the
    CEO's retirement is in the offing) to a focused discussion
    of succession and development efforts;

    • developing with the CEO goals related to succession and
    management development to be achieved each year; the
    CEO's efforts may be tied to his or her incentive compen-
    sation (discussed in greater detail in chapter 7).

2. As a result of these regularly scheduled management development sessions with the CEO, the board should have an up-to-date and clear picture of the process by which the company is identifying and developing future leaders as well as specific individuals and their development.
3. The board should have plenty of exposure to aspiring leaders, in business as well as social contexts, so that they can help monitor their development.
4. Once the succession culture is developed, the board will want to explore with the CEO ways to retain executive talent by providing appropriate financial, psychological, and organizational rewards.

An important element in establishing a succession culture that cultivates leaders from the bottom up is the relationship between the board and the CEO, which is something we discuss further in chapter 5.

5

Striking the Right Balance
Between the Board and the CEO

"It's illusory to view a [corporate] board as a school board where everyone is equal and all groups in the community are represented. The CEO's judgment has greater weight than anyone's on the nominating committee and his voice should be louder than anyone else's."

—Irving Shapiro, former chairman and CEO,
E. I. du Pont de Nemours & Co.

When it comes to choosing a successor, where does the CEO's responsibility end and the board's begin? To what extent is director involvement essential in ensuring that future corporate leadership is developed, and at what point does it become meddling? How much autonomy should a CEO be allowed before it becomes a matter of the board shirking its responsibility? Where is the proper boundary between management and governance? Trying to answer these questions requires recognizing that the relationship between the CEO and the board is as complicated as any in the corporate world.

All that has been written and said about the role of independent outside directors lately might lead one to believe that the cozy past relationship—characterized in its most extreme form by a domineering CEO surrounded by top managers and crony CEOs from other companies there to do his or her bidding—has been replaced by outsiders with no personal or professional ties to the CEO. The truth, depending on the individual company, of course, may lie anywhere along this spectrum. While the trend is toward more independent boards—and most leading companies' boards are composed of a majority of outside directors—there remain many exceptions.

In this chapter we examine the shifting dynamics of the board/CEO relationship: how it was viewed traditionally, how it is changing, and, perhaps most important for our purposes, the optimal balance to achieve between the board and the CEO to promote the most effective succession planning efforts. As we have throughout the book, we use company examples to help illustrate best practices—in this case, what the CEO and the board, working separately and together, can contribute to the process.

How "Independent" Are Independent Directors?

It is now an accepted tenet of good corporate governance that boards should have a preponderance of outside directors. According to the 1999 Spencer Stuart Board Index, the trend toward director independence is firmly entrenched: Seventy-eight percent of directors at the one hundred leading companies we surveyed in 1999 are outsiders.

Outsiders, however, are not necessarily unknown to the CEO. The governance universe of large public companies is surprisingly small. When boards look for other CEOs, still the most sought-after group for directorships, they will very likely look at those candidates who head companies of comparable size in a related industry. Given these customary parameters, it is not surprising that most of these CEOs will know each other, and perhaps have become good friends. A number of CEOs have told us that some of their closest friends are on their board. Yet these "friends" are also expected to keep tabs on the CEO, evaluate his or her performance, and fire the CEO if necessary.

A look at who is actually seeking and hiring these independent directors reveals another inherent rub in our governance system, a conflict that militates against the ability to build true objectivity into the board process. Corporate governance systems have evolved somewhat differently in each country, depending on historical tradition. In the United States, one of the constants has been, and continues to be for the most part, CEOs who are also the chairmen of their boards. This means, in reality, that CEOs are most often directly involved in the selection of new directors, and when they are not that they can have great influence over those charged with this duty.

Once asked to join the board, these outside directors, more than likely selected by the CEO, are then expected to do an about-face and act as guardians of shareholder interests. Directors are caught in a bind because of the conflicting nature of their duties. They feel a natural loyalty to the CEO who may have selected them, whom they may have worked closely with for some time, and who may even be a personal friend. On the other hand, directors increasingly feel the weight of their fiduciary responsibilities as boards are regularly singled out by institutional shareholder groups, aided by the press in their efforts to push for greater company performance and to dispense with CEOs who appear to be thwarting that effort.

One way around this built-in conflict, it has been argued, is to promote a more independent board by splitting the chairman/CEO function between two people, creating an independent outside chairman, along the lines of the predominant model in the United Kingdom. Though shareholder activists and others have pushed for this "reform" at various times, however, it has never become institutionalized as a common practice in the United States, and is primarily used during transitional or particularly turbulent periods. Apparently the concept of an independent outside chairman is not something that generally can coexist comfortably with the dominant American business culture. In a country accustomed to having one boss in charge—"the buck stops here"—the concept of a separate chairman and chief executive is a tough sell.

To push for the independence of outside directors, some boards—according to the model formalized by General Motors in "Board Guidelines on Significant Corporate Governance Issues" (1994)—have appointed lead directors (sometimes one for the entire board, sometimes different ones depending on the issue at hand). In our opinion, though, this can create something of a board within a board, where outside directors may meet with each other and sometimes with other top managers without the participation of the CEO.

In extreme cases this sort of arrangement can put a real strain on the relationship between the board and the CEO.

Within the context of greater outside director independence there are a couple of recent trends we view as positive and healthy. In the past several years it has become increasingly common for outside directors to meet without the CEO to discuss controversial issues. Not surprisingly, the tenor of the conversation may change completely if the CEO is present. We endorse this practice as long as information is shared quickly with the CEO. Many CEOs, in fact, also endorse this practice, and a number of CEOs and directors we have spoken with recommend a meeting of outside directors as a routine part of each board meeting. In this way such meetings are less likely to be viewed as going behind the back of the CEO, and any issues that arise can be discussed and resolved regularly.

Another way in which independent directors have been showing more muscle is by undertaking performance appraisals of the CEO. This is an important trend, but board compensation committees must take care to ensure that the measures they are using to evaluate the CEO are consistent with the goals of the business. Moreover, if the CEO seems to be falling short, it is important to make sure that his or her performance is being compared with industry competitors, not the entire S&P 500. Such an evaluation should be multidimensional—not merely stock-based—and should include the strategy agreed on with the board compared with industry norms.

The Way It Was

In our business, where we deal with succession-related matters every day, we see close up and firsthand the difficult dynamics of the board-CEO relationship. We not only recruit CEOs and other top managers to companies, we also recruit outside directors for boards, so we have learned to appreciate the roles and conflicts on both sides of the equation. The human drama we have witnessed at the top of these large and influential organizations runs the gamut from CEOs turning on directors, to directors turning against other directors, to CEOs getting caught in the crossfire. So what works and what doesn't? What is the proper balance between CEO and board, contribution and control that companies should strive for in succession planning?

Clearly the traditional approach, where the CEO has sole responsibility for designating and grooming his successor and deciding on the timing of the transfer of power, is an idea that most boards are no longer comfortable with, although the process still operates much like this at far too many companies.

Irving Shapiro—formerly chairman and CEO of E. I. du Pont de Nemours & Co., now retired from that post for sixteen years, and of counsel to Skadden, Arps, Slate, Meagher & Flom LLP in Wilmington, Delaware—has an interesting perspective on the old versus the new when it comes to CEOs and boards. "We never had a problem on the subject of succession," observes Shapiro. "DuPont has always had an elaborate process for measuring talent." The current CEO, for example, was spotted as a potential leader when he was in his early thirties and groomed for the CEO spot. The company's six VPs on the executive committee were by definition the stars of the company and the group from which the successor to the CEO would come. "But the company wasn't told of my choice until the time came to announce my successor. Until then, the jury was still out," remembers Shapiro.

In addition to his longer-term choice, Shapiro also planned for possible crises that might have rendered him unable to function as CEO. "I advised a senior member of the board that in case of emergency, 'X' could be my successor, and the choice might change over time."

Shapiro talks about how he took DuPont from an inside, inbred board of "old-timers" to a board that included outside directors. In the early days, as Shapiro puts it, there was no nominating committee, and the search for outside directors was very much the responsibility of the CEO. Shapiro was committed to a more diverse board, and his efforts resulted in the first minority, a former governor of the Federal Reserve, and the first woman being appointed to DuPont's board.

Without a formal director selection process in place, how did

Shapiro identify outside directors for DuPont's board? His primary resource was what he referred to as "the fraternity of CEOs," where the business and social lives of colleagues who were also large-company CEOs would frequently intersect, providing informal opportunities for CEOs to help sort out each other's problems. A former CEO of AT&T, for example, provided a lead on a woman with a strong public relations background who did end up joining DuPont's board. "The grapevine works," says Shapiro. Of course, these appointments did need to be approved by the board, but in his experience, the board "always approved the CEO's recommendations."

Shapiro characterizes as "foolishness" some of the current corporate governance guidelines that have been promulgated by various groups, particularly those that focus on independent directors as a separate faction that is there to serve as a check to the CEO. "It's not possible for a company to run well if there is an adversarial relationship between the board and the CEO," states Shapiro. "The board either has confidence in the CEO or not. If not, that has to be resolved; if so, the board has to let the CEO do his thing." What is more, he says, the board should never confront the CEO and risk humiliating him at a board meeting. Anything vaguely critical of the CEO should be discussed privately with the CEO, not in a board meeting.

What happens, we wondered, if the CEO and the board don't concur on the urgency of succession planning? "If the CEO doesn't want to retire," Shapiro says, "doesn't want to pick a successor, and is prolonging the agony for everyone, a single senior director should have a private talk with the CEO and tell him that he needs to get a replacement ready. There's always a small group of directors who deal with sensitive issues; they are key people. But it needs to be managed in a discreet fashion—you don't embarrass the CEO."

Shapiro sees little sense in separating the CEO role from that of the chairman. "The CEO is the only one who knows all the relevant facts about the company," he says. "If you make the CEO subservient to someone on the board, the facts are still funneled through the CEO. The CEO is the captain any way you want to parse words, so it's just as well if the CEO is also the chairman of the board." Shapiro believes that newer governance models promoted by various groups—in his view, chiefly by people who have never served on boards—tend to elevate form over substance. Though he admits that there have been vast changes in corporate governance over the past twenty-five years, he believes that common sense has to be the controlling consideration. Directors will naturally look to the CEO for his wisdom, and the directors' main function is still to support the CEO.

AT&T: A Wake-up Call for Boards

Shapiro's views typify the CEO side of the traditional CEO-board relationship, but far from being a thing of the past, it is surprising how many boards are still constrained by these traditional roles. Even with shareholder activists and the media breathing down their necks, we believe that far too many boards still relinquish most responsibility for succession planning to the CEO.

In terms of evaluating the influence of directors, the influence of the CEO, and the proper balance to strive for in the succession process, it's worth looking at AT&T Corporation, where succession served as a wake-up call for boards. Fair or not, this case became a very real symbol of what can go wrong when boards abdicate their responsibility.

As a longtime CEO, Bob Allen had earned the absolute trust and confidence of the board. When the board asked Allen to undertake a search for a number two who would eventually succeed him as CEO, he went about the task in good faith and sought to come up with the best-qualified successor. Typically, when a board is happy with the CEO's and the company's performance, the CEO will select the number two. In the case of AT&T, however, the media had been scrutinizing the company for some time. Performance of the company had been slipping, and the general sentiment in the investment community was that Allen should be replaced.

At this point the board members should clearly have communicated to Allen their intention to get involved in selecting a successor. They should also have let Allen know that he might be leaving ahead of schedule. The board should have been aware of its responsibility to

intercede and take control of the succession process at this point, particularly given the fact that Allen had already chased away two very
able successors: James Barksdale, former CEO of Netscape Communications, Corp. and now managing partner of the Barksdale Group,
and Alex Mandl, CEO of Teligent, Inc. But despite all of these warning signs, the board remained on the sidelines.

When the board was presented with a slate of highly qualified candidates, John Walter, CEO of R. R. Donnelley & Sons Co., emerged as
a finalist. Directors unanimously approved the choice of Walter, naming him president and COO in October 1996, with a specific timetable
for promotion to CEO. But, saying he "lacked intellectual leadership,"
the board subsequently refused to name Walter as Allen's successor,
prompting his resignation in July 1997. These developments
prompted other significant players to bail out as potential successors
to Allen as it became clear that he was not at all ready to step down.

After Walters' resignation, the board assumed responsibility for
selecting Allen's successor and in December 1997 elected C. Michael
Armstrong, formerly CEO of Hughes Electronics Corp., CEO of
AT&T. Since he has taken over as CEO, Armstrong, a highly capable
executive, has added billions of dollars in market capitalization to
AT&T.

Are Boards Overcorrecting?

We believe that there has been a bit of an overreaction by boards and
that the pendulum may be in danger of swinging too far in the other
direction—that is, from a totally CEO-managed process that allows
for little board input, to one that is totally controlled by the board,
with little input from the CEO.

In fact, we have observed a dramatic change in our business since
these developments at AT&T, a change that reflects a growing fear of
boards that the CEO will control the succession process. To further
follow this line of reasoning, if the CEO controls the succession
process and if the process fails, directors will be exposed for abdicat-
ing their fiduciary responsibility to the company. According to the

worst-case scenario, investors, led by institutional shareholders, lose faith in the company, make a public show of pulling out their investments, and go elsewhere.

The fall 1997 search for a successor to James Unruh, Unisys Corporation's longtime CEO, serves as a good example of this drastic shift in attitude by a board. It happened that the Unisys CEO search, for which we were also retained, began just about the time Walter announced he was leaving AT&T. Our initial meetings with Unisys's board regarding strategy and process for identifying Unruh's replacement clearly conveyed the message that Unruh would play a pivotal role in the process. The board recognized that Unruh had been a capable CEO, but determined that the company needed a successor who could take the company to "the next level."

Following Walter's resignation from AT&T, the Unisys board suddenly had a complete change of heart and began to focus on "our responsibility," essentially taking the process away from Unruh. In fairness, the board was also under a great deal of pressure, with the stock under siege by institutional investors. With management removed from the process, Spencer Stuart served as the de facto staff to the board in the search for a successor. Recognizing the inherent weakness in management being completely divorced from the process, we sought, and were granted, permission from the board to keep Unruh up to date on the process and to solicit his opinion on potential successors. In great measure the input from Unruh consisted of information on market conditions and company issues—areas we had to understand thoroughly to attract candidates and execute the search properly.

Working with a strong board and with the critical input of the CEO, we did help Unisys attract an excellent CEO to succeed James Unruh—Lawrence Weinbach, who had spent his entire career at Andersen Worldwide and who had served as managing partner and chief executive since 1989. With a broad-gauged financial services and marketing background, Weinbach has proven a good match for Unisys, which, since he has taken over as CEO, has been among the top twenty corporate performers in stock appreciation.

The Envelope, Please

Not long before his retirement in January 1998, Frank Cahouet, CEO of Mellon Bank Corporation, met with us to discuss succession. At first glance, Mellon Bank also appeared to one of those companies where succession matters are still strictly within the domain of the CEO. Once a year for nearly a decade, Cahouet carefully planned for his own demise. He delivered a sealed letter to the head of the board's compensation committee, outlining his choices for the next CEO. "I would give my suggestion as to who should replace me if I were to fly into a mountain tomorrow, as well as those who were emerging as successors if I went through to normal retirement," Cahouet told us.

The letter, of which Cahouet also kept a sealed copy, was to be opened only in the event of a crisis that would prevent him from continuing to discharge his duties as CEO, and so, in the course of his nine years in the position, it was never opened. Each year, the unopened letter was returned to him by the head of the compensation committee, and Cahouet promptly replaced it with another, sometimes with the same succession choices, sometimes with different ones.

Upon first hearing of "the letter," one might think, "this is a guy who has the board wrapped around his finger." Yet, in spite of the fact that Cahouet, like most CEOs, apparently has a healthy ego, the purpose of the letter was not to issue an unchallengeable edict on precisely who his successor should be. Cahouet's intention, it turns out, was completely the reverse. Why the shroud of mystery surrounding Mellon's CEO succession process? Cahouet's explanation was a simple and sensible one: "I didn't want the board to be influenced by my opinion until they had to be—I wanted them to have a chance to make up their own minds about potential successors."

None of the choices Cahouet recommended in his letter during the past nine years would have been either a surprise or a stranger to the board. The board and the CEO did, in fact, collaborate closely on the succession process at every stage, and the board was routinely exposed to the eight vice chairmen who collectively comprise Mellon's uppermost layer of management. Cahouet's successor, Martin

McGuinn, formerly vice chairman of retail financial services, was a member of this group.

By carefully planning with the board, Cahouet helped to ensure that a capable CEO was ready to take the reins at Mellon. His list of succession choices evolved during his tenure, changing to reflect shifts in company strategy and prevailing economic conditions. And each time he submitted his recommendation, he put forth more than one candidate, leaving the board the option of selecting the successor whom they deemed better able to take on the CEO's duties at a particular time. "I would try to work out a combination of two people," Cahouet explained—"for example, someone who is strong on the technical side of the business, who is able to break down complex issues, versus someone who has good instincts, is warmer, and knows everyone." Cahouet was fully aware that his contribution to the process only went so far, however, and that the final decision was in the hands of the board, which, although it was likely to concur with one of his choices, was in no way bound by them.

The Governance-Management Boundary Line

Mellon Bank, like most of the companies we met with for this book, has a fairly predictable and easy-to-define line between the role and responsibilities of the CEO and those of the board. The process seems to work best when both sides respect each other's boundaries, with the CEO not venturing too far into the governance area and the board not interfering in the actual management of the company.

To Mackey McDonald, CEO of VF Corporation, a $5 billion retail company, that boundary is not a fuzzy one, but clear and distinct. "I don't think the board plays a role in the execution of succession plans," he says. "It's the board's job to make sure a plan is in place, but if directors think it's their job to train the next CEO, that could make things very difficult. Assuming the CEO is performing properly, it's his job to develop the plan for succession and develop the candidates and present them to the board."

In the case of VF, it is interesting to note that when McDonald was appointed CEO in 1996, the former CEO, Lawrence Pugh, remained chairman for two years before McDonald took on both roles (a topic we discuss in further detail in chapter 9). McDonald readily admits that this arrangement isn't for every company. But splitting the CEO and chairman functions worked at VF because cultivating an effective relationship among the CEO, the chairman, and the board has been a high priority for all involved. "When it doesn't work," McDonald says, "it's because the chairman and former CEO doesn't release enough information, or the new CEO isn't secure enough to have someone looking over his shoulder." One thing has to be "crystal clear," however, McDonald emphasizes. Though a lot of people may have input into key decisions, when it comes down to making a decision, everyone has to recognize and respect who the decision maker is.

The board at SmithKline Beecham, the Philadelphia-based pharmaceutical company, goes further than most in its direct involvement with key management. The company follows a practice that clearly works for SmithKline Beecham but that could prove risky for others from the point of view of cultivating an effective CEO-board working relationship.

At SmithKline Beecham the board has strong, established links with the company's corporate-management team, whom it meets with once a year in a joint meeting to review the strategic direction for the company. Over the course of three days, the combined groups focus on key business issues and have the opportunity to nurture what has proven to be an extremely effective working relationship. An outgrowth of these meetings has been the practice of assigning board members to specific functional and geographic areas. This "adopt a region" policy enables the directors to increase their involvement and understanding of aspects of the company they have not been exposed to and "marries" them—according to Daniel Phelan, SmithKline Beecham's senior vice president and director of human resources—to the succession planning process.

While many companies would find this relationship between the board and top management too cozy for comfort and actually counterproductive, because of the chemistry of key players at SmithKline Beecham, this approach appears to work well. Moreover, since the company does have a separate chairman, based in London, and CEO

Jan Leschly, based in Philadelphia, individual directors serve as important vehicles for the chairman, who is a significant distance from headquarters, to receive steady input on the members of the management team.

A less-secure CEO or a more intrusive board could easily turn this practice into a disaster for the company. Another CEO's back might readily go up at the mere prospect of directors being directly involved in managing the company, particularly at distant subsidiaries, completely out of sight of the CEO. A case could be made that the board is treading on the CEO's turf and undermining, even usurping, his or her authority. Leschly, however, is comfortable with this approach and sees it as a valuable component of the overall succession process. Directors certainly do have the opportunity to evaluate, at close range and in the trenches, the performance of the top-management team.

Another CEO we spoke with, who heads a major pharmaceutical company, reflected on how the CEO-board relationship has evolved, and points to the increased interaction of directors with top managers who are not on the board to illustrate what he considers the positive and constructive trend toward independent, involved directors. The changes he has implemented at his own company—and he sees similar changes at other companies—have resulted in more of a team effort between the CEO and the board, in contrast to the past relationship, which was much more carefully staged and controlled by the CEO.

"We have definitely moved away from the board meetings where we stuck to formal agendas," says the pharmaceutical CEO, who prefers to keep a low profile and thus not be directly quoted. "In the past, board meetings were highly predictable, with committee reports and things the board needed to take action on. There was no room for open discussion, and under those circumstances it's tough for directors to understand the challenges facing the company and work as partners with the CEO. Board meetings now tend to focus on business issues, so directors have the opportunity to contribute their own experience and know-how."

According to this CEO, there is clearly more involvement, which he welcomes, from the board in key areas such as succession strategy and other strategy development. This approach requires a lot more work by directors, but the company stands to gain a great deal from their involvement. "In the past," says the pharmaceutical CEO, "when the CEO may have been working, for example, toward a major capital investment or acquisition, everything was neatly laid out for board approval." In contrast, today, he says there is advance notice of the strategy and policy implications, and sufficient time for directors to consider proposals and provide input, what he calls a "no surprises" approach. Similarly, when it comes to succession planning, directors are expected to be involved at each phase, not to sit back and wait for the CEO to announce his or her plans.

Toward a More Balanced Approach

Despite the success of CEOs such as Leschly and McDonald—who have established strong bonds and excellent working relationships with their boards—the board/CEO relationship remains an uneasy one at many companies. In light of AT&T's events and steady pressure from institutional shareholders and the media to act as guardians of the company, boards are justifiably afraid of the criticism they will encounter if they allow the CEO too much control over the succession process. In the "overcorrection" we will surely find that a process that is controlled by the board is not likely to be any better, and perhaps worse, than one managed solely by the CEO.

But most boards we have worked with have designated some role for the CEO in the selection of a successor. Indeed, assuming a CEO has done a good job, who better deserves the board's trust and confidence? Presumably the CEO knows the company inside and out: He or she sees management perform daily and should be best able to evaluate future potential for leadership. Board members, on the other hand, have never run the company, do not possess the CEO's intimate knowledge of the business, and have full-time jobs elsewhere. The best approach is to resist the temptation to overreact to incidents such as AT&T's and for directors to resolve not to let outside pressure cloud their judgment. Although there is no one prescription for every company, succession should be viewed as a 50:50 partnership between the board and the CEO.

Surely there is an appropriate role and an opportunity for significant input from a number of sources in the succession process: CEO, board, and outside purveyors of expertise. And it is crucial to define the roles and boundaries—what each can uniquely contribute, and potential pitfalls if any party to the process goes beyond the bounds of its responsibilities—to achieve the proper balance that will yield the best results.

A Circumscribed Role for Search Firms

On the subject of possible pitfalls that may undermine the relationship between the board and the CEO and possibly warp the process, we would like to briefly discuss what we see as the most effective role for search firms. This may seem surprising coming from a search firm, but we believe that many companies have gotten into the habit of involving search firms inappropriately in the succession process, often beyond the extent to which they should be involved, without recognizing the downside of this approach.

The burden of responsibility for succession planning that was for years delegated to CEOs must be the province of the board, with input from the CEO. Search firms are increasingly used by boards as a tool to cast the widest possible net to include both internal and external candidates. But search firms should never be delegated the responsibility of making the ultimate succession decision—that is clearly up to the board. As the pendulum has swung to more active—and at times excessively cautious—boards seizing control of succession, there is a tendency for boards to see search firms as a panacea for all that was wrong with the CEO-manipulated process of the past. According to this reasoning, the search firm, as objective outsider, is better able to identify and assess CEO successors. The limitation here to be wary of is that, in spite of any protestations from recruiters to the contrary, search firms introduce their own set of biases into the process, primarily a bias toward recruiting outsiders. Moreover, search firms—even more than directors—are part-timers, mere visitors to a company. They can't possibly possess the in-depth knowledge of the business and individual managers' capabilities as the CEO who lives with them day in and day out.

As active boards have begun to eclipse the responsibility of management in the process, the role for search firms has correspondingly increased. There is certainly a danger in seeing the contribution of search firms as a substitute for the valuable input that can only come from the CEO. Of course, we believe that search firms can and do play a vital role in the process, but it is important to keep in mind that we represent a resource that should complement, not take the place of, a company's own resources.

Succession Planning for Directors

Of course, one of a company's most important resources is its board. Much of a company's success in succession planning goes back to the point with which we began this chapter. Boards must comprise a group of strong, independent directors, each strategically selected for what he or she can uniquely contribute to a specific company. That brings us back to the question of how directors are chosen. In fact, succession planning is as important in shaping a company's governance body as its management team.

The traditional approach to recruiting directors, and still followed by many companies today, was articulated by Irving Shapiro, DuPont's former CEO. According to this approach, the CEO worked the CEO grapevine for leads on directors. In addition, many boards were heavily populated by the company's top managers, direct reports to the CEO. Often the choice of a new director made by the CEO and rubber-stamped by the board was a fellow CEO, a close friend and colleague of the one whose board he was to join. This inbred system frequently led to interlocking directorships—"you scratch my back, I'll scratch yours"—now considered a big no-no by advocates of progressive corporate governance principles. But the fact is that a situation where the CEO is surrounded by directors who are either friends or direct reports will likely be short on objectivity and critical feedback.

A number of companies—including leading high-performing ones—have recently been criticized for maintaining this insular approach to corporate governance. Though quadruple heart bypass surgery in 1994 raised the specter of succession for Michael Eisner, CEO of the Walt Disney Company, the matter has yet to be publicly resolved at the company. Amid criticism from institutional investors that Disney's board is unimpressive, unprofessional, and ill equipped to deal with the complex issues facing a major company—including succession—the company has lost three potential successors in the past few years, and there is no obvious heir apparent to fill Eisner's shoes.

Eisner, who was quoted in an August 1997 *Business Week* article on succession as saying, "I am fifty-four years old and if it hadn't been for my bypass, no one would be even talking about succession," is decidedly missing the point. Even assuming he is in the peak of health, he, like other mortals, could still fall victim to an accident or sudden illness tomorrow. It is unfortunate that Eisner seems unwilling to confront succession, despite all that is at stake for Disney, and that his board is unwilling or unable to push the matter.

The more enlightened and far more common approach now to constructing a board is to have a nominations committee composed of outside directors who are charged with the responsibility of identifying—on a regular basis, not merely when there is a board seat opening up—capable directors who can contribute to the board. Increasingly there is a trend to identify those who bring a skill or a particular type of experience to the boardroom table that is otherwise lacking, such as a background in technology, marketing, or international.

Changing Boards Will Change Succession

Practical considerations, including a shortage of CEOs to serve on boards, also have necessitated the shift in mentality from "Whom do we know?" to "What do we need?" in recruiting directors. As the responsibilities and performance of directors have been more closely scrutinized over the past several years, the media and shareholder activist groups have highlighted examples of what they have perceived as abuse and incompetence, often where individuals—particularly "professional directors"—may have overextended themselves by sitting on more than a few boards. This exposure has led to calls for restrictions concerning the number of boards an individual should be permitted to sit on.

In addition, mounting challenges at global companies that operate on a twenty-four-hour-a-day business clock have demanded that CEOs maintain their focus on their own company. CEOs would formerly sit on as many as five boards, but now typically sit on only two to three at the most. In our experience, companies are increasingly limiting the number of outside boards on which CEOs and their direct reports may serve. And it is now customary for our clients, who all want to ensure that they attract focused and committed directors, to ask us to exclude from consideration any active executive who is already serving on more than two to three outside boards. This is a relatively new criterion that we have noticed emerging over the past several years and is now almost universal.

Currently boards are experiencing something of a generational change. The old guard, who may have served on a handful of boards, are retiring. They are being replaced by new directors who, because of these new restrictions, must pick and choose their board opportunities much more carefully. Many boards, including a number we are now working with, have several directors retiring over the next few years, which adds to the time urgency in finding new directors.

We believe that the current "shortage" of directors will ease over the next several years as companies increasingly recognize the value of a more diverse board, defined by type of experience, in addition to ethnicity and gender. The definition of the ideal director is already beginning to change from the traditional "active CEO" to include those who can contribute experience and expertise in a range of other areas. Because of their unique perspective, CEOs will, of course, continue to be in great demand as directors. But we are seeing a growing need for directors with a broad business perspective who bring other critical skills to the table, including executives with backgrounds in technology, who can help companies understand the impact and the competitive advantages of rapidly changing technology. In addition, given our global environment, companies are now serious about finding directors with significant international experience. Prospective directors who possess these skills and experience do exist in increasing numbers.

Mackey McDonald, CEO of VF Corporation, describes his company's system for recruiting directors who will be valuable resources for the company: "We try to make sure that we maintain on the board directors with a range of experience and functional responsibilities, who can provide substantial input into key decisions. We work with a profile and look for directors who can fill areas we perceive as gaps. It's important to add people with new perspectives to the board."

Far from being threatened by the presence of more independent directors who are not an established part of the CEO's inner circle, the more secure CEO will view the newer breed of director as enriching the board. During our many conversations with CEOs and directors, both in the course of our client work and while gathering information for this book, a number have mentioned to us the importance of broadening the board's horizons by adding this independent element. Thomas Horton, former head of the American Management Association, who serves on corporate boards as well as that of the National Association of Corporate Directors (NACD), says that, in his experience, "the most valuable director is often the one who is least close to the business, but is simply intelligent and knows how to ask the right questions."

This shift in the composition and modus operandi of boards—which is a reflection of the dramatically different way in which boards plan for their own succession—will surely have a profound impact on many fundamental corporate processes, including that of succession. More independent directors possessing a greater range of viewpoints, experience, and expertise will want to be real, contributing partners at every phase of the succession process.

A School for Directors

For directors to become real partners with the CEO on succession and other vital processes, they must have the knowledge and skills to deal with myriad issues. As we discussed earlier in this chapter, the traditional approach to serving as a director required little more than being a friend of the CEO and following his or her lead. Now boards are expected—indeed, required—to take a much more active role in their companies than ever before, but many may not be equipped to do so. Viewing issues from the perspective of one's own experience is not enough anymore; directors need to be aware of various approaches to dealing with issues. What most often leads to success? What approaches have been tried that have been less successful? Companies can no longer afford the luxury of allowing directors time to get over the learning curve when the board may be confronting critical, time-urgent issues demanding attention.

Our daily contact with CEOs and directors convinced us that there was a gap that needed to be filled in directors' training. Newer directors need to get up to speed on the basic responsibilities of a director; moreover, novices and veterans alike need to become adept at taking on and executing duties that directors were never before expected to handle.

When we sat down with dean Thomas Gerrity and vice dean Robert Mittelstaedt, Jr., at The Wharton School to create a program for directors, we considered the many new issues and responsibilities boards are facing, how we could broaden the perspective of directors, and how we could best equip them to meet these challenges. Among the many issues we wished to address was, of course, succession planning.

We wrestled a bit with the structure and format such a program should have. The traditional lecture-style approach did not seem suitable either for the high level of executive we would be attracting or for the range of experience of directors, from first-time to seasoned. Moreover, our goal was not to develop an academic exercise, but a realistic executive program that would mirror, as closely as possible, what actually goes on in the boardroom. After considering a number of possibilities, we agreed that a "living" case was the best vehicle to expose participants to the widest range of issues in the most true-to-life setting possible.

Now five years old, the Directors' Institute has held ten sessions and has been successfully exported to London as the Directors' Forum, where MegaMicro, Inc., the fictitious company that forms the basis of the living case, is MegaMicro, plc. Judging by the response we have gotten to the program—in terms of the number and level of participants as well as positive feedback—it appears that we are fulfilling our mission of providing directors with the tools they need, as we believe no other program currently does, to actively contribute to their boards.

Lewis Platt, former CEO of Hewlett-Packard, who served as the CEO of MegaMicro for a session of the Directors' Institute, told us "some of the most important discussions we had during our session at the Directors' Institute focused on having the right mix of skills among directors. Fortunately for everyone, the days when everyone expected the CEO to provide all the answers and directors to merely sit around the boardroom table nodding their heads are long gone. In today's complex businesses and markets, it's a foolish CEO who doesn't recognize the need to have first-rate directors who want to be actively involved and can provide the expertise in a variety of areas that can enhance the vision of the CEO and the decision-making capability of the entire board."

Because we are aware that directors often lack the tools and experience to deal effectively with CEO succession, a succession scenario is often included in the three-day program. At the December 1998 session of the Directors' Institute, for example, succession reared its head at the final board meeting of MegaMicro. Though we had written this into the program because we realized that many directors had little experience dealing with succession, it came as a surprise to MegaMicro's board (except for MegaMicro's chairman and CEO, James Hardymon, real-life CEO of Textron, Inc.) and the audience in the theater-in-the-round.

At the start of the board meeting, the chairman left to take a phone call, then returned, announcing to the board that he had gotten some bad news: Test results indicated a serious health problem. He then indicated that he was too distraught to run the board meeting and asked the board to carry on without him.

It soon became obvious that MegaMicro's board hadn't planned for the possibility of a CEO who might die suddenly or become incapacitated, but working under the assumption that they should expect the worst, they scrambled to establish a priority list of tasks: Did they have an immediate successor? What directors might comprise a succession committee? How could they immediately disclose the information and assure investors that things were well in hand?

Judging from the audience's reaction, we would guess that there wasn't a director there who wasn't affected by the experience and who didn't go back to his or her primary company and outside boards and say, "We have to make sure we're prepared for the unexpected." Valuable take-homes included how to organize the board and plan in the midst of a crisis, but, even more important, how to take the proper steps and plan ahead of time so that the board doesn't have to scramble when disaster strikes. Indeed, in our analytical discussion after MegaMicro's board meeting we covered a number of board best practices relative to succession planning, which had suddenly taken on new meaning for these directors after experiencing a true-to-life succession crisis. We discussed, much as we have throughout this book, planning for a range of possible scenarios (sudden death, long-term retirement); designating a chairman in the event of a crisis; and regularly getting enough feedback from the CEO on immediate successors so that a plan can quickly be implemented in an emergency.

Board Checklist

Most boards, given their druthers, would certainly prefer not to wait for a crisis before acting on succession. Establishing the proper relationship with the CEO will help to ensure that such issues are addressed in a calm, logical, and timely fashion. As we've seen, achieving the right balance in the relationship between the board and the CEO is tricky, but absolutely essential to effective succession planning. Our board checklist for chapter 5 includes some things directors should bear in mind regarding their relationship with the CEO as well as their duties as directors:

1. Is your board truly an independent board with a preponderance of outside directors?
2. Have the board and CEO established succession planning as a collaborative process?
3. Is the board ready and able to prod the CEO to discuss successors and retirement if the CEO doesn't recognize the urgency?
4. Does the board actively seek regular discussions with the CEO on possible succession candidates and their readiness to succeed, both short-term and longer-term replacements?
5. Do directors observe the proper boundaries and focus on governance-related matters, or are they interfering with the management of the company?
6. Does the board rely too much on outside experts such as search firms on succession matters to provide information and judgment that should more appropriately come from the staff?

While the board's relationship with the CEO is critical to succession planning work, so, too, is the relationship between the board and next-generation CEOs. Ongoing exposure to the group comprising prospective successors is clearly a best practice. The better directors get to know potential candidates in a variety of business and social settings, the better informed a decision they can make when the time to pick a successor finally comes. Establishing an ongoing relationship between the board and likely heirs apparent is a major focus of an effective succession plan and one we explore in detail in the next chapter.

6

The Delicate Matter of the "Number Two"

"Timing and the lack of a clear message about succession played a major role in my decision to leave AT&T. There were no promises that I would be CEO, but I was clearly on the path to the next job. Then, much to everyone's surprise—certainly mine—the CEO announced that he was going to stay another four years. The notion of working in that situation was not appealing."

—Alex Mandl, CEO, Teligent, Inc.

As we noted in the previous chapter, the relationship between the CEO and the board is a tricky one to manage. Equally delicate and critical to the success of succession planning efforts is the relationship between the CEO and potential successors as well as the relationship between potential successors and the board. In this chapter we explore the complexities of these relationships and what works and what doesn't. Companies that tread carefully when it comes to number twos send strong messages to their organizations about how executives are valued and are consequently much more likely to hold on to talent.

A company's ability to retain a talented and experienced number two depends on dealing with several factors that seem to have an impact on an effective CEO–number two relationship, including:

• the satisfaction of the number two in his or her position;

• The ability of a number two who had been passed over to come to terms with the improbability of becoming CEO, as well as the ability to forge a constructive relationship with the "winner";

• clarity around the issue of timing, including when succession will take place, and what assurances (verbal, titular, and financial) the number two expects to receive and when.

These are significant issues that, if handled improperly, may have a negative effect on the entire company's well-being. They should not be left to the CEO and the number two to sort out; board awareness and involvement are crucial. It is important for directors to examine how they can effectively manage the number two's part in the succession process. The board must determine whether it is being given sufficient opportunity to get to know potential successors and see them in action in order to make an informed decision about succession. Directors must also consider the consequences of various approaches to succession: whether there will be a clear designated successor well before the top slot opens; a horse race among a few top contenders; or a wide-open field where a broad range of candidates are considered, including prospects from outside the company.

This chapter is intended to offer perspective on these issues, clarify some of the factors that help a company maintain a number two's loyalty, and provide a sense of the kind of relationship that the board, the CEO, and the number two should seek to build.

What Makes for a Great "Marriage"?

While he was number two at GE, Lawrence Bossidy is reputed to have described his relationship with CEO Jack Welch in the following way: "Jack gets to do whatever he wants and I get to do whatever is left." This story, related by Kevin Sharer, president and COO of Amgen, Inc., who will asccend to CEO in May 2000, illustrates how not to keep the COO happy. Though they were close friends and colleagues—described by Sharer, who knew both while at GE himself as "the best management team on the planet"—Bossidy did ultimately leave for the top spot at AlliedSignal. While Bossidy clearly had a major operating and strategic role at GE, his lighthearted comment may have been a more accurate reflection of his inner feelings than people imagined. His remark also highlights an important challenge: how to ensure that the number two has a satisfying job—satisfying enough so that he or she won't be lured away by competitors.

Many number twos would agree that a key element in maintaining their satisfaction is how their territory is defined, if it is defined at all. As with the vice president of the United States—the ultimate number-two job—some may wonder if there is a real job or whether the position is purely and simply a CEO-in-waiting. An ill-defined job that is viewed as merely picking up after the CEO, or treading water until the CEO is ready to step down, is a surefire recipe for corporate discontent and larger succession problems down the road.

If they are not satisfied with the scope of their responsibilities, talented and ambitious number twos will likely leave when the right opportunity is dangled in front of them—especially if they are not getting clear and positive signals from the CEO about the timing of a future transition, Sharer says. "COOs have to view their current position as one of professional growth, and there has to be some light at the end of the tunnel indicating when they're going to be the next CEO. Otherwise the bodies will fly off the bridge at a pretty good rate."

After having considered what doesn't work, what does make for a good "marriage" between a CEO and a number two? One of the most important factors—according to many number twos we have spoken with—is whether there is a clearly defined job that entails a significant range of responsibilities that he or she can "own," manage, and develop, rather than merely being viewed as a subordinate to the CEO on a daily basis. Successfully managing a sizable portion of a large company brings with it the opportunity for wide recognition. Someone with the drive, ambition, and talent to be CEO needs not only the work but also the visibility and credit that go with doing a big job and doing it well.

Kevin Sharer says that in his current position at Amgen "the CEO was smart enough to carve out something day-to-day where we don't talk and don't have to. He is also secure enough to publicly allow the number two to be seen as an important player."

Establishing a positive relationship between a CEO and a number two can be challenging enough. It is especially difficult when the two individuals had been in competition for the CEO position. John A. "Fred" Brothers, executive vice president of Ashland, Inc., is familiar with the experience, having been through a CEO transition in 1996 when a competitor was awarded the top spot.

Despite his initial disappointment of having come so close only to lose out on becoming CEO, Brothers was able to bounce back and successfully work as part of a close team with his former competitor, the new CEO. Without this sort of resiliency by the unsuccessful candidate in such a contest (if he or she remains with the company), the ongoing relationship can never be productive. In Brothers' own words, "If you're going to stay around, the first thing you have to do is get over the fact that you're going to be number two and not number one. If not, there will never be a good marriage."

Joining forces for a common goal can also forge a strong relationship between competitors, especially if the CEO and the number two successfully manage to share responsibilities. Brothers experienced that shortly after the succession when dissident directors at Ashland launched a proxy fight. "In late '96 and into '97 we had our hands full," Brothers says. CEO Paul Chellgren dealt with the governance issues while Brothers managed several major deals the company was trying to complete. In this case, a positive working relationship was strengthened by the fact that the CEO and the COO were united in fending off a threat, helped by a clear division of labor with enough substantive responsibilities to create demanding jobs for each of them.

Visibility Before the Board

One obstacle to boards being able to properly discharge their duties with regard to succession planning is that directors often have insufficient exposure to number twos. With little knowledge of the skills, experience, and personal chemistry of potential successors, it is difficult for directors to realistically assess a candidate's readiness and suitability for the CEO job. When all information on potential successors is filtered through the CEO, the board cannot get a real feel for the people it may want to consider for the top job when the time comes.

How can a board expect to assess potential CEOs without an opportunity to get a clear sense of how they think and operate, both in a high-pressure business context as well as in more low-key social situations?

"It's critical for boards to demand visibility of the top three, four, or five people," says Alex Mandl, CEO of Teligent Corporation and former COO of AT&T. "Secure CEOs do this on a regular basis—they're proud of their teams and want the board to see them. Unfortunately, there are CEOs who are not secure and do just the opposite. They dominate their boards, they read all the reports. This is a board responsibility, though, and directors have to lay it on the table. They have to come right out and say, 'We want to see more of your top-management team. We want exposure to the key people who make decisions around the company.' The board can make it happen, and they have the right and the responsibility to do so. Otherwise, if the CEO says to the board, 'If something happens to me, I want so-and-so to be my successor,' the board's reaction should be, 'Compared to what?' The board has to have ongoing, regular exposure to potential successors as well as reports from the CEO on their progress."

The opportunity for directors to interact with potential CEOs is an important part of the selection process. At Rohm & Haas, a specialty chemical company, where the original candidate pool of four was eventually whittled down to two, Raj Gupta, CEO since September 1999, says that he and his final competitor for CEO were involved in every board meeting, except for discussions regarding compensation. "The board had every opportunity to get to know us both socially and professionally, and the CEO did not stand in the way; he was willing to take a backseat."

If the CEO erects a barrier between directors and potential CEO successors, however, it may not be easy for the board to surmount it.

"There's a board I sit on and the other directors include a lot of CEOs. I was new to the board and felt we weren't seeing enough of the CEO's team," says Sharer. "Finally, one day I said to the CEO, 'We need to get to know your guys better.' He didn't get it! We only were getting to see them in scripted presentations for maybe twenty minutes, six times a year. It's the board's job to get a dialogue going, but it's really hard to do."

Directors have to prod the CEO to provide access to the top executive team, and they must be prepared to be persistent about it. Otherwise they may find themselves in a situation where the CEO recommends a successor whom they have no basis to assess and no alternatives for comparison.

Clarity of Message Is Key

Alex Mandl was widely acknowledged to be Bob Allen's successor at AT&T, but the understanding was more implicit than explicit. Mandl had received no clear signals about a transition, and timing was not discussed. One day he picked up the *Wall Street Journal* to learn that Allen had decided to postpone his retirement, originally scheduled for his early sixties, until age sixty-five. Four years seemed a long time to wait, especially when there was no certainty that Mandl would eventually become CEO. Mandl decided to leave, accepting a position as CEO of Teligent, a wireless communications company that was so new it was still nameless when he was hired.

Mandl's departure from AT&T provides an important lesson for any company that fears the loss of top talent. An otherwise successful CEO-COO team may begin to fall apart as the time for the actual succession nears if the COO does not receive some clear signals that he or she is the chosen successor and understand precisely what the timing will be for the transition.

"I had a great relationship with Bob during most of my tenure at AT&T, we had very defined roles. At the end things got confusing and awkward," reflects Mandl.

As a former second-in-command, Mandl is not alone in calling for clarity in the succession process. Most number twos expect to be told well in advance about their prospects of becoming CEO and the approximate timing of the transition. But John Drosdick, president and COO of Sunoco, Inc., is prepared to put forward a case that people in his position are not entitled to know exactly when or even if they will get the promotion. "What if the world changes in a year and you don't get it? The other side is that you are hired to do the job you do. Why are you necessarily entitled to know about the future?"

Michael Levine, former executive vice president, marketing and international, Northwest Airlines Corporation, has a quick answer to that: "Because the job has been dangled in front of you from day one. It's not fair to expect someone to live with that sort of uncertainty and be prepared to stick around indefinitely."

Making it clear to a number two when a transition is likely to take place and whether he or she is likely to get the nod is not only a matter of courtesy and respect for the number two, it is also the most logical way to safeguard a precious resource: a capable executive in whom the company has invested and who will provide valuable continuity. It is amazing to us how many executives with tens of millions of dollars at stake in a company will talk to us when we are conducting a search on behalf of a client. Financial handcuffs, while they may give someone pause, are not a foolproof way to hold on to top talent. People who are left hanging in the balance and given no clear signals about the succession path and their role in their company's future are particularly vulnerable to being hired away.

Although the issue of when a CEO will actually step down is a sensitive one—often difficult to discuss and more often avoided entirely—communication between the CEO and potential successors is possible. Before Rohm & Haas announced that Raj Gupta would succeed J. Lawrence Wilson, there was a great deal of anxiety between the top two contenders. According to Gupta, the "not knowing" was the most difficult thing to deal with. "I realized that the timing is tricky in announcing a transition, it's either too soon or too late. But we [Gupta and J. Michael Fitzpatrick, the other contender for CEO] told Larry a couple of years before his retirement that we had to know if we were in the running. We decided that we would rather deal with the individual disappointment than continued uncertainty."

Communication was facilitated with the help of the top human resources executive, who served as an intermediary, allowing the primary parties to maintain some distance but still remain informed. "We had an understanding and a system worked out with her that proved very useful," Gupta says. "If we had a question related to the transition, we would ask her and she would plant it with the CEO." The CEO in turn would close the loop by getting back in touch directly with either of the two potential successors who had posed the question.

Sometimes a CEO may feel there is a valid business reason for not providing clarity as to when a successor will be chosen. The CEO that Sharer reports to at Amgen, Gordon Binder, felt he couldn't give a date too far in advance. "The day I announce my retirement and successor, I'm a lame duck," he had said. That could leave the number two wondering, says Sharer, "Should I talk to the board about it and try to get some clarity from them? I've got an incomplete message here."

In the final analysis the board has to help manage the CEO–number two relationship and ensure that the right messages are being conveyed to a potential successor at the right time.

The Board Should Take the Lead

One of the things we have learned from conducting high-level executive searches is that potential successors who feel they have not gotten a clear message from the CEO or the board regarding their own future are much more likely to listen to outside offers and much more at risk of being recruited away.

If the CEO seems prepared to stall indefinitely on naming a successor and establishing the timing of a transition, then the board must step in and more directly manage the process. "The board has two ways that it can go," says Sharer. "It can either say, 'We'll keep our options open to the last second' and delay making a decision on the successor, or it can say, 'Good CEOs are hard to find; let's make sure he (or she) doesn't get away.'"

How and when specific succession plans will be communicated is a critical issue for a board to discuss and resolve. "The board needs to have a serious discussion," says Mandl, who advises giving the nod to the chosen successor rather than keeping him or her dangling and risk losing the talent. "Do we agree that he's the person?" he says, putting himself in the role of a director. "If so, why are we not telling him? It's essential that the board agree on this point. If the person sits there and doesn't hear from the board, it could be awkward. One phone call and he could be gone."

What if a CEO is reluctant to establish a timetable for transition or orchestrates a succession plan that leads to a potential successor leaving the company? At some point—preferably sooner rather than later—it is the board's responsibility to take on the unpleasant task of confronting a CEO.

"Someone who is viewed by others as a lead director," says Sharer, "and there's one on every board, and everyone knows who that person is, has to talk to the CEO and make it clear how important it is to the board that the company not lose a valued number two."

Fred Brothers relates a story about a board on which he serves, where directors had to have just such a confrontation with the CEO. "About two years before his scheduled retirement, the CEO told us that he had selected his successor from the two candidates who were in the running. In the CEO's absence, the board took an informal vote on the two candidates, and it was unanimous that the board wanted the other candidate. We spoke directly with the CEO, helped him to change his mind, and began to put the process in place with the title change."

To avoid a confrontation with the CEO it is important for the board to think about the issue in advance and make its views known in a timely fashion. "When the CEO started down the path with this one candidate," says Brothers, "the directors were too timid to challenge the CEO and we let him continue. Finally, as the signals to this candidate [that he was the chosen successor] got stronger and we didn't believe he was the right choice, we felt we had to step in. But we should never have let it get that far."

Keeping a Good Number Two Who Loses the Race

A smooth transition requires not only a "great marriage" between the CEO and the number two, but also a cooperative working relationship among the contenders for the top spot. Raj Gupta uses his own recent experience to illustrate this point.

Culture runs deep at Rohm & Haas, where managers tend to come, build careers, and stay. Gupta describes the transition from one CEO to the next as a succession that had been "very competitive," but mellowed to "collaborative and friendly" in the final stage. The civilized tone for the final transition was set by longtime CEO Wilson, according to Gupta. "He had been through a horse race himself. The number two had stayed in spite of the intense competition that had persisted throughout the succession. Larry was cognizant of the fact that he didn't want the next generation to go through what they had been through."

How did Gupta and his number two competitor avoid falling into the trap of divisiveness and jealousy that so often results from this sort of competition? "There is a mutual respect between Mike [Fitzpatrick, president and COO] and myself," says Gupta. "I've been with the company for twenty-six years, he for twenty-two. We're both highly competitive, we both wanted to be CEO, but we discussed how we could have a fair contest. Are there two jobs going forward in the company? we wondered. We also agreed that if we both stayed, we wouldn't stand in each other's way. There would have to be both a place and sufficient challenge for both of us."

As things turned out, Fitzpatrick will run the core business of Rohm & Haas, which makes up two-thirds of the company, and the technology function. Gupta will run the remaining third of the company and the governance function. "We have distinct, well-defined roles, and each plays to our strength. In addition, the board allows for two insiders—the CEO and the COO—so we'll both serve on the board."

"We haven't lost an outstanding executive from the company," Gupta says. "A strong internal culture like ours probably self-selects against people who are driven only by compensation."

Not all horse races end so amicably. For those that don't, how effective are financial handcuffs in stemming the flow of top talent from a company, especially during the final stage of a CEO succession when companies are particularly vulnerable?

Michael Levine believes that at the top levels of corporations it is not generally the financial pull that helps one company retain executive talent or another company attract it. "The real issue is, can you accommodate this personality and can he or she give up the opportunity to be number one? Those companies that are successful in retaining number twos are those where the CEO is secure and can provide the public exposure and ego opportunity to ensure that people stay. Handcuffs of the financial kind only work with people who are not financially independent."

But given the growing mobility of executives in general and the wealth of opportunities for them, corporations are increasingly inclined to use options and restricted stock to attempt to keep a tight hold on experienced leaders.

Brothers says that his handcuff package, made up of restricted stock to vest after seven years, was "certainly a factor" in keeping him at Ashland. "I wouldn't say it was decisive. I'm financially independent, but the arrangement did give me a sense of comfort. I've been approached for CEO positions elsewhere. If there were no financial payout, I may have walked away."

Most number twos would probably agree that these financial handcuffs do not provide any guarantees that valued executives will remain with the company if they lose out in the race for CEO. But if such measures give executives pause and make it harder for them to walk away, these arrangements are probably well worth having.

Ongoing Dialogue and Assessment with the Board

If a board gets to the point where it is concerned about having "the succession discussion" with the CEO, things have gotten out of hand. We mention this in other contexts in other chapters, but it bears repeating now as we wrap up some of the major issues covered in this chapter: Succession is far more than the CEO merely stepping down and his or her successor taking over. It is an issue that goes straight to the core of a company's values on the development of leadership.

Some CEOs, many of whom we profile in previous chapters, begin their term with an understanding with the board that one of their key responsibilities will be developing leaders throughout the organization and successors at every level. They relish the leadership-development role and the opportunity to showcase before the board the talent they have had a hand in developing. Others refuse to share the limelight with anyone and resist viewing the leadership of the company as anything that extends beyond or below them. These are obviously not the organizations that become hothouses for executive talent.

As we have noted, the composition of the board helps to determine how direct it is in dealing with and reassuring successors. Boards with operating executives, perhaps because they better appreciate how difficult it is to secure a capable CEO, are more likely to try to preserve stability than financial executives, who are more removed from day-to-day operations. But experienced number twos continually emphasize how important it is for the board to manage the succession process.

Board Checklist

The following list highlights some of the board's major succession responsibilities with regard to number twos:

1. From the very start of a CEO's tenure, boards must establish a pattern where up-and-coming leaders, especially potential successors, have frequent exposure to the board in a variety of business and social settings so that directors can assess their progress.
2. Directors' knowledge of the management team should be from direct contact, not filtered through the CEO.
3. Directors should ascertain—in their interaction with both the CEO and potential successors—whether those next in line are deriving enough personal satisfaction and recogni-

tion from their job. Have areas of responsibility been clearly carved out, and is the CEO willing to share both important responsibilities and glory?

4. If succession is on the horizon, has a clear timetable been established and communicated to the successor, including the timing of title changes and handing over responsibilities? The board has to be willing to hold the CEO's feet to the fire or risk losing valuable talent.

5. The board should implement appropriate financial handcuff arrangements to encourage potential successors to remain with the company.

Because succession can be such a hit-or-miss proposition if is left entirely up to the individual CEO, it is critically important that the board establish and adhere to a well-thought-out and predictable process. If all participants in the process know what to expect and when, results are far less likely to depend on the whims or personal preferences of any one individual.

As we briefly touched on in this chapter, for an executive who might be considering leaving a company, financial handcuffs can help to tip the balance in favor of him or her remaining. In chapter 7, "Financial Tools That Promote Succession Planning," we discuss some of the latest thinking regarding financial tools for the three primary parties involved in succession planning—CEOs, potential successors, and directors—and what can be done to help ensure their commitment to the succession process and optimal results.

7

Financial Tools That Promote Succession Planning

"Look, to an owner of a business, the most important thing is who's managing the business for the owner, and the key in succession is finding someone capable to manage your enterprise. . . . Equity ownership makes you think like an owner. As an owner, you're going to take charge, take a lead in the process. Why? Because you're protecting your investment. Bad succession means low profits."

—Charles Elson, professor of law, Stetson University

Succession is a complex process, as we have observed, and there are several different parties to the process—the sitting CEO, number twos, and directors—all with very different roles to play. In previous chapters we have discussed some of the ways in which companies can help ensure that CEOs and boards will devote the needed time and energy to succession to create a reliable process. In addition to some of the factors we've already discussed—such as establishing regular timetables to identify and nurture talent as well as review the progress of potential successors—the right financial framework, with different incentives applying to each party, can help to establish a sound and orderly succession process and keep things on track. Just what those incentives should be and the philosophy underlying each is the subject of this chapter.

From the point of view of the interests of the corporation, there should be a number of ongoing contributions from key parties:

• The current CEO should be regularly involved in keeping track of the career progression of likely successors and finding appropriate ways to further their development. He or she must be aware of up-and-comers and must help to assure their ongoing value to the corporation.

• Number twos, likely CEO successors, should have a commitment to rounding out their skills and experience in appropriate ways. There will also be a waiting period, which will vary widely by company, before an heir apparent is named. Companies are eager to find ways to retain the services of these individuals before, during, and after this transitional period.

• Directors need to constantly be kept in the loop regarding the development of promising successors, help keep the CEO's feet to the fire regarding his or her own succession responsibilities, and replace the CEO if necessary.

To increase the likelihood that all parties will perform in ways that will create the best ultimate outcome for the corporation, there are financial incentives as well as disincentives that apply to CEOs and to number twos. Moreover, there is a new philosophy taking hold regarding the compensation of directors that our research indicates is much more effective from the viewpoint of representing shareholder interests and overall director diligence.

Linking Succession Planning with CEO Compensation

How do farsighted directors ensure that the CEO's compensation encourages commitment to the succession process? How do they translate expected performance into the right dollar figure? They start by recognizing the importance of succession planning as well as the fact that bonus compensation can play a role in keeping the CEO focused on it. These boards understand why developing and selecting a successor can be difficult for a CEO, and they construct the most appropriate financial incentives to help counter these most human and predictable of tendencies.

Carl Weinberg, an executive compensation specialist with Price-waterhouseCoopers, says that "for successful CEOs, succession planning is one of the most difficult, emotional issues because it forces them to face their own mortality. The more successful the CEO, the more difficult it is."

What can a board do to encourage a CEO to push ahead with a task he or she would just as soon put off? One obvious step is to examine the company's approach to CEO compensation and determine what incentives they can build in to move succession as a priority up the agenda.

First, some perspective on the overall issue of CEO compensation. Increasingly, leading companies are defining the CEO job in terms of a few key areas of responsibility. They determine the CEO bonus based on performance in those designated areas, and success in achieving specific objectives worked out with the board the previous year. The process is a continual one, and we frequently work with boards and compensation committees to design pay packages that promote key organizational goals that have been identified by the board and the CEO. Some companies even use a specific formula, perhaps dividing the incentive compensation into thirds or quarters to correspond to agreed-upon primary responsibilities.

Weinberg calls CEO performance appraisals "the most important tool to increase the effectiveness of succession planning." Many boards conduct performance appraisals of the CEO much as they would assessments of employees throughout the organization, setting out specific objectives and ways of achieving them.

Given that succession planning is becoming widely recognized as one of the CEO's most fundamental responsibilities, it logically follows that a CEO's diligence in performing this duty should play a major part in any appraisal determining CEO compensation. The practice of appraising the CEO's performance in this way, and linking it directly to compensation, gathered considerable momentum during the 1990s, partly because of recommendations by the National Association of Corporate Directors (NACD).

What does it mean to be a successful CEO? What tasks should one accomplish, and how should success be measured? When it comes to succession planning—sometimes paired with a more general and deeper-reaching concept such as "management development"—it generally means carefully monitoring the career development of candidates who are the most likely successors to the CEO, providing them with opportunities to acquire and demonstrate new skills, and keeping the board well advised on this process. It means ensuring that there are potential successors prepared to step in immediately, and a fresh generation of leadership further along the horizon, depending on the age of the CEO.

How does it work in practice? For one approach, let's take another look at Hercules, whose commitment to long-term CEO succession planning was described in chapter 1.

Hercules pursues a continuous organizational development process based on the concept of "critical position competencies." The position of each person in the company is defined in terms of critical competencies: the skills and experience they need, and the responsibilities they must execute.

Hercules applies the same principle to its CEO. At the start of each year the board negotiates with the CEO to determine eight to ten critical areas of accountability. At the end of the year, he is assessed based on how well he has delivered against these overarching objectives. And this assessment has a direct impact on his bonus. "If, for example, the CEO were about ready to retire and he had not hit target goals for grooming successors and developing a succession plan he could take a major hit on his bonus," says former human resources head Edward Carrington.

Similar processes are in place at other companies where the importance of long-term succession planning is recognized. At GTE, the bonus of CEO Chuck Lee has been based on three to seven priorities worked out with the board at the start of each year. One of Lee's five priorities each year has related to people and leadership development, which includes succession planning. At SmithKline Beecham, which will undergo a CEO change in April 2000 (when Jan Leschly is replaced by COO J. P. Garnier), succession is clearly understood by all parties to be one of CEO Leschly's top priorities, along with creating shareholder value and achieving growth objectives. "There is direct linkage of CEO compensation and his articulation of a succession plan," says senior vice president for human resources Dan Phelan.

Positive incentives are the common currency of the succession process. But in some cases boards may find it necessary to use both the carrot and the stick. For example, a board may simultaneously freeze the CEO's salary and offer a larger option grant as a reward for achievement in the succession process. This two-tiered approach sends a "message about how vitally important a task this is," says David Leach, executive vice president of Compensation Resource Group.

As a CEO approaches retirement there is naturally greater urgency regarding the readiness of candidates. A board may even specify the specific number of qualified candidates it expects the CEO to have fully prepared for the top job, with a time frame established and part of the CEO's bonus riding on the results.

Raymond Smith, who stepped down as CEO of Bell Atlantic at the end of 1998, explains that his board had very specifically spelled out his responsibilities for succession toward the end of his term, linking the CEO bonus with succession planning. Working with the head of the board's human resources committee on succession and executive development, Smith was expected to come up with a specific number of candidates against which his own performance on succession would be evaluated. "I should have had four candidates groomed and prepared," he said. "I succeeded in having three—I felt three was a B+."

Number Twos: Carrot vs. Stick

Dealing with the number two in a corporate succession is a double-barreled challenge: Companies face the pivotal task of preparing likely successors and keeping them in place, while retaining the loyalty of disappointed contenders. This group comprises a significant repository of executive talent—as well as an investment by the company—that no organization can afford to alienate or mismanage.

Financial incentives can send powerful signals to number twos about their future prospects, how highly they are valued, and what areas they should focus on to enhance their chances for promotion. The right signal can make the difference between keeping a number two or losing one, between maintaining enthusiasm and killing it.

David Leach of Compensation Resource Group observes that corporations see holding on to their number two as a renewed priority, given that "many companies feel increasingly vulnerable when it comes to losing talent, and realize they need to do things to retain their people and send a message that these people are important and that they want to hold on to them."

Companies can send strong signals about what and whom they value through their compensation practices. A company that has anointed a successor ahead of time, rather than set up a horse race, has the opportunity to smooth the transition process by integrating compensation strategies for the CEO and the CEO-in-waiting. Such an integrated strategy takes into account the shift in responsibility from the CEO to the successor. "We would develop a timetable and chart the evolution of responsibilities over time, and outline from a philosophical standpoint how both pay packages would evolve," says Carl Weinberg of PricewaterhouseCoopers. "At a certain point, when the outgoing CEO has handed over enough key responsibilities to the successor, the CEO's compensation would actually go down." For the heir apparent this is a reassuring signal, offering a concrete indication that the CEO is serious about handing over the reins and demonstrating that the transition is moving forward according to an established timetable.

Performance appraisals for the CEO and the heir apparent can also be coordinated, with the goals for the CEO, including development of his or her successor, while the number two's goals focus on career development and addressing any shortfalls in skills and experience needed to succeed to the top.

Holding on to a potential CEO is crucial, but it is made easier by the anticipated promotion ahead. But what if that promotion to the top spot isn't to be part of a candidate's future? How does a company deal with an excellent candidate who is nonetheless destined to remain number two rather than move into the big corner suite? What signal should the company send in that situation?

Honesty is crucial. "If being number two is not within the career prospects of the individual, you serve yourself and the organization well by being candid," Weinberg says. "You're also sending a very important message to those in the next two levels on how people are treated."

If the organization wants the executive to stay, it is important to outline a career-and-reward strategy, especially if he or she is starting to think about retirement. Ego and money are very much intertwined, and the size and type of the reward package will go far to communicate the organization's sincerity and commitment.

"Handcuff" arrangements are among the most commonly used tools to discourage top-level people from leaving a company. What are the most effective methods of handcuffing? Leach believes the best course is usually to offer long-term incentives, generally constructed with stock options or restricted stock.

"Stock options are granted at the curb price when they're given and usually have a term of ten years on them," Leach explains. "Companies will often put restrictions on these in terms of vesting requirements, usually that the person has to be there a certain length of time before the stock vests. Of course, the stock price has to go up for them to exercise their option."

For even greater insurance in holding on to key executives, a company can offer restricted stock, which is often part of a hiring package. "The idea is that you're given a grant of stock, but you can't sell the stock for a certain period—usually three to five years," Leach says. "The advantage of restricted stock is that it is immediate ownership. Typically you can vote the stock and receive dividends, you just can't sell it."

One disadvantage of restricted stock is that it is more costly than stock options from an accounting standpoint. From the shareholders' perspective, a bigger drawback is the fact that restricted stock incentives provide executives with a financial reward that is not linked to performance. How the stock performs in the market does not determine whether the executive profits, only by how much. "The stock price could go down and it would still have value because they're not putting up any money, they're just receiving the grant of stock after some passage of time," Leach says. "With the options, stock price has to go up for there to be value." Based on this consideration, stock options more closely link compensation to shareholder value because if the stock price goes up, the shareholders and the executive both gain.

For an experienced number two who has yearned to be a CEO and is ambitious about getting to the top, it is entirely likely that no financial incentive can compensate for not getting the chance to reach the pinnacle of the company. But the right incentive may help to keep them on the bench where they are needed. Given the shortage of proven top-level talent, that must be a corporate priority.

Making Financial Tools Conform to the Tax Code

Companies seeking to construct compensation packages to reinforce succession planning efforts, or other organizational goals, need to take into account one of the newer wrinkles in the tax code.

In 1992, while seeking the presidency for the first time, Bill Clinton promised to seek an amendment to the tax code that would prohibit corporations from taking tax deductions for compensation to a CEO in excess of a million dollars per year. A year later Congress passed an amendment to the tax code creating Section 162M, which applies to CEOs and a company's executive officers—those listed in the proxy statement. It states that any compensation to these individuals in excess of a million dollars will not qualify as a tax deduction unless the compensation is performance-based.

To corporations, their boards, and their accountants, the qualifying phrase "performance-based" is of critical importance. But how precisely is that interpreted when it comes to compensation? By definition, salary does not qualify. Value realized upon exercise of stock options would qualify as long as the plan fits certain criteria approved by shareholders and administered by a committee of outside directors, among other requirements. Compensation received as a result of a bonus program would qualify only if the bonus program fit certain criteria. The program, for example, must be approved by shareholders and administered by a committee of outside directors. Moreover, the bonus plan, as approved by shareholders, would have to be specific about what performance measures are to be used and how the bonus is to be calculated. In practice, another individual should be able to take the same formula and reach the same calculation. The test for deductibility is that the calculation be based strictly on objective measures of performance.

As Weinberg explains, "If part of a CEO's incentive compensation is based on something like 'We've developed a really good succession plan,' that's judgmental and would not qualify as tax-exempt income under the revised code."

What if there had been clear guidelines for a CEO spelled out with the board at the beginning of the year? If, for example, according to board-established objectives, the CEO had developed three successors and has been training them in a specified number of ways to help them develop whatever skills they might need to ultimately take over the CEO's job? Would incentive compensation based on the achievement of these objectives qualify?

"Probably not," responds Weinberg, "It's a stupid rule. Essentially it's got to be financial formulas. So what would qualify? An earnings-per-share objective. Or a market share. You could even do a customer satisfaction index, as long as there's a formal process for calculating that. The idea is to take judgment out of the equation. That's really what it's about. So things like developing human capital for the long term, and how well you're doing that, is judgmental. And that's what they're trying to avoid. What some companies have done to get around this is they've created in their bonus program what's called negative discretion. So, in other words, the formula produces a number, a bonus number. The compensation committee can always approve a smaller amount and then that's kosher under Section 162M. So what these companies do is they've got a formula amount and they've got a real program, and the formula amount basically expresses the maximum you can get, on all the judgment factors.

"The formula produces an inflated number. Say you've got a bonus that based on this formula could pay as much as a hundred thousand dollars, just to make up a number, so you're going to get somewhere between zero and a hundred thousand . . . based on how you perform according to these judgment factors. That's okay under the tax code because the formula expresses the maximum."

Considering these obstacles in the tax code, the bull market of the past several years, and the desire of many companies to retain executives and reward longer-term performance, it is not difficult to understand the popularity of stock option grants.

"More companies are linking succession planning efforts to the size of option grants," Weinberg says. "They might say something like, 'We're not satisfied with your efforts so we're giving you forty thousand options instead of a hundred thousand,' or 'You did a good job: You identified three or four candidates, you set rigorous development programs for them, we're going to reward you with a hundred thousand instead of forty thousand.'"

Making Directors Think Like Owners

The impact of financial tools ultimately depends on the people who have the job of wielding them—the board of directors. As we have described throughout this book, directors are the key players in making sure that the field is tilted toward long-term planning in the succession process. It is the directors who must keep the succession process on track and ensure that decisions promote the overall interests of the shareholders. It is the directors who must approve the financial incentive plans described in this chapter and determine how well the CEO has earned them.

What is the most effective way to ensure that directors fulfill these responsibilities to the shareholders, and keep their interests continually in the forefront? In our experience, the vast majority of directors are intellectually and philosophically committed to the principles of fiduciary responsibility and independence. But, in reality, directors and CEOs form personal bonds that may affect directors' judgment. Indeed, directors usually owe their position to the CEO. How can a company use financial tools to ensure director independence in the succession process?

We examined this issue in depth in preparing a report titled "Director Ownership, Corporate Performance, and Management Turnover" (June 1998), which went to the heart of the issue of director performance and compensation as overseers of management. But before describing the study and its conclusions, it would be useful to set the stage by discussing the evolution of the corporate board of directors, particularly as it relates to effective corporate leadership.

Boards of directors evolved as a solution to an inherent problem in the corporate structure: the separation of ownership and management. In earlier times, as now, the primary responsibility of directors was management oversight for the benefit of residual equity owners. At one time it was relatively easy to ensure that boards represented the interests of shareholders, because traditionally boards were made up of the business's largest shareholders. Substantial shareholdings by directors acted to align board and shareholder interests and to create the best incentive for effective oversight. Indeed, directors were not even allowed direct compensation for board service.

By the early 1930s, in the largest corporations, the board was no longer the dominion of the largest shareholders. The American economy had grown by leaps and bounds, and corporations were far more than local ventures owned, controlled, and managed by a handful of local entrepreneurs. Instead they had become national in scope. This increase in complexity and scale led to the rise of a professional management class to run these far-flung corporations. In addition, as these rapidly growing enterprises required greater and greater capitalization, they were increasingly owned by many thousands of smaller individual investors, but no shareholder group owned enough stock to dominate the entity. Professional managers moved in to fill this control vacuum, and boards, rather than being filled by representatives of shareholder groups, were populated by individuals who had been handpicked by management and had little or no shareholding interest in the company.

In recent years the disengagement of directors from shareholders and their identification instead with management has prompted criticism by shareholder activist groups and the media. Heightened scrutiny has been focused on ineffective boards that ignored warning signs and failed to dispose of underperforming CEOs until after their companies sustained significant damage. We posited in our report on director ownership—and we believe most would agree—that the primary responsibility of the corporate board of directors is to engage, monitor, and, when necessary, replace company management.

How do we encourage them to do that? How do we reinstitute the board culture in which directors are sufficiently independent of the CEO and properly motivated to consistently represent the interests of the people who actually own the company? We believe there is a relatively simple answer to that question: To encourage directors to think like owners, they must be compensated like owners. Equity ownership is crucial. The findings of our research support the premise that directors will do a more conscientious job of monitoring the performance of the CEO, and replace him or her when necessary, if their financial interests are aligned with those of the shareholders.

None of these findings surprised Charles Elson, professor of law at Stetson University, with whom we collaborated on the above-mentioned report. For many years Elson has been a highly vocal advocate of supporting the director-as-owner mind-set.

While there is not a wealth of empirical evidence, we believe that paying directors in stock encourages them to think and act like owners, including taking an assertive role in succession planning. Our view is based on personal experience, anecdotal evidence, intuition, common sense, and the practices of many leading companies.

Some companies are adopting innovative ways of encouraging equity ownership among directors, such as giving them multiples of options based on the amount of stock they buy. One company with which we are familiar allows directors, each year, to convert their cash retainer on a 3:1 ratio for stock options. Under this formula, for example, a thirty-thousand-dollar retainer can be converted to ninety thousand dollars' worth of stock options at the market price. This practice, which grew out of the LBO environment, is a sensible way to encourage directors to own stock and to tie their efforts to the long-term interests of the company.

In some cases, companies are going beyond stock compensation for directors, and requiring them to purchase stock in the company from their own pockets, with a minimum entry requirement. These affirmative equity entry requirements are not intended to close the door to anyone who does not possess great wealth. It is as important a symbolic gesture as it is a financial one, a way of saying, "I have confidence in this enterprise, and I want to be part of it. I'm putting my money where my mouth is." When we see companies—and there are many of them—where directors have invested virtually nothing of their own money, we have to wonder about the strength of their commitment to the future of the company.

But how big an investment should directors be expected to make? At what point does a threshold become a barrier? Is there a magic number that will ensure that directors will be sufficiently motivated to monitor management?

"Personally, I feel it ought to be around a hundred thousand dollars," Elson says. "For some reason, the empirical data that I've gathered to date indicates that. It was big enough that it made a difference; it was small enough, on the other hand, that it didn't wipe anyone out. In other words, it was an attainable goal for almost any director. If you said a million dollars, that's not attainable, but a hundred thousand dollars, even for an academic, is an attainable goal. For some reason, I don't know why, that number makes people pay attention—maybe it just sounds like a big number, that's something for the psychologists to figure out—but for some reason, we see a divergence at about a hundred thousand dollars."

One practice that discourages ownership thinking on boards, retirement plans for directors, is rapidly dying out. In our annual board survey—the Spencer Stuart Board Index (SSBI)—we note that for 1999 only 6 percent of companies queried now offer retirement plans for directors, down from an astounding 79 percent only five years before. There is also a strong undercurrent from institutional investors who believe directors should not receive compensation or perks in any form that encourages them to identify with management as opposed to owners. That is good news for shareholders who want to be represented by independent, involved directors, as opposed to those who just go with the flow.

Elson, for one, is happy to see perks such as retirement plans phased out: "The problem with those plans is that they end up rewarding director longevity rather than director activity. And in rewarding longevity, you probably can make a case against activity. In other words, the closer you get to divesting that benefit, the less likely you are to rock the boat for fear of losing that benefit. And when you think about it, serving on a board is not a job you retire from, it's not a job in that sense. You're a fiduciary for your shareholders, you're representing your fellow shareholders. A pension suggests you're an employee—it really puts you in totally the wrong mind-set."

The trend lines in director compensation—including a larger component made up of stock, and all-stock retainers on the rise—point in a clear direction: directors being paid like owners, not like hired hands. It is not a very big leap from that foundation to the desired result: directors who demonstrate greater independence and recognize the crucial role they play in succession planning. Companies that have altered their director compensation packages are sending a clear message that directors will no longer be rewarded for merely showing up at meetings, filling a seat, and hanging on until they retire from the board.

Director-Owners Discharge a CEO

When it comes to arguing that directors/owners are crucial to an effective independent board and a proper succession process, few CEOs have been as outspoken as Albert Dunlap. One might even say that he was hoist with his own petard, because he ultimately lost his own position at the top of Sunbeam Corporation as a result of his own philosophy put into action.

"Boards exist to serve the shareholder," he told us when we interviewed him about a year before his June 1998 dismissal. He made a number of similar remarks, for which he had become well known in corporate America, indicating that he was the champion of the share-holders and that their interests should reign supreme: "I'm the leading advocate of good boards in America. Most boards are woefully inadequate." He frequently repeated his mantra about the importance of stock ownership for management and directors.

According to Dunlap, under his stewardship at Sunbeam, senior executives, himself included, received no bonuses and no salary increases, only stock. Directors received no pension, no meeting attendance fees, only stock (and reimbursement for meeting expenses). In addition, directors were required to own a minimum of five thousand shares in order to serve on the company's board.

In response to the oft-expressed argument that such requirements lead to companies having only rich people serve on their boards, Dunlap was unequivocal: "When people say that, I tell them, 'They have a new thing—it's called a bank, where you can take out a loan if necessary to buy the stock.' When directors are tied to the performance of the company you can bet they'll care about succession."

Ironically, it was this Dunlap-instituted policy—mandatory investment in the company by directors—that may have helped to save Sunbeam by encouraging the board to act expeditiously when it lost confidence in Dunlap's ability to lead the company. Though the stock had jumped when Dunlap's appointment was first announced, it began to drop precipitously after only a short time. The directors, including Charles Elson, who had all paid a stiff price of admission to join the board, took quite a hit.

Thinking like owners and identifying with the interests of share-holders, the board finally believed it had no choice but to discharge Dunlap. The fact that many of the directors—Elson included—were also friends of Dunlap's made the task that much more agonizing. "It was horrible," Elson reflected. "I never want to go through that again. But I'll tell you something. The equity ownership certainly played a big role, I'm convinced, for all of us, because we all were feeling the same loss and we were concerned. Had we not had that kind of equity and it had simply been a fiduciary duty, well . . . it's very easy not to push the button on the CEO. There's every reason for not moving."

Clearly, requiring stock ownership as a tool to align directors' economic interests with the interests of shareholders achieved the desired result in the case of Sunbeam. The directors identified with the shareholders they represented, not the CEO who appointed them. As Elson describes it: "Our alignment was with the company itself, and our role was to continually monitor management. And when we felt that we had reached the point we no longer had confidence in management, then we made a change, and that's really what it came down to."

The right incentives can help induce directors to stand up for shareholder value, even if it means siding against a friend and colleague; they can prompt CEOs to put their heart and soul into preparing for a succession, even if it means accepting their own ultimate dispensability; and they can encourage number twos to submerge their own ego, as well as focus on the areas in which they need to improve their skills.

Board Checklist

Our board checklist for chapter 7 suggests how can boards use financial tools to encourage all participants in the process to properly and effectively play their role:

1. When designating specific areas to be given weight in CEO performance appraisals, assign a high priority to succession planning and to involving the board in that process.
2. If an heir apparent has been officially designated, consider linking his or her performance appraisal and compensation formula to the current CEO's, and revising compensation to reflect changing responsibilities.
3. When a strong number two has been turned down for the position of CEO, determine the priority of retaining him or her, and adjust compensation accordingly.
4. Devise handcuff packages tied to profitability, and timed to ensure the executive's retention through an extended transition period, long enough to provide the new CEO with the support required and to ensure leadership stability.

5. Structure CEO and number-two bonuses to meet the "performance-based" criteria required under the revised tax code.

6. Move toward significant director share ownership, primarily through director compensation in the form of equity; move as far as possible from compensation arrangements that treat directors as employees (such as directors' pension plans).

Financial tools, properly targeted, can encourage all key participants in the succession process to fulfill their proper roles. While it is important for directors to focus inward on implementing their succession agenda, they must also keep an eye carefully trained on the outside, as we discuss in chapter 8 on global intelligence®.

8

Global Intelligence®:
A Window on the World

"You can never do too much 'diligence.' We can certainly do the financial diligence, product diligence, customer, distribution, and manufacturing diligence on the company. It's also essential, however, that you research and take a good look at the backgrounds of quite a number of the senior executives, even midlevel executives, in an organization. And a company is really selling itself short if it's not digging deep to determine what the culture of the company is and what the background of the individuals are who will be asked to carry out a lot of these things that are going to be part of the synergies of the diligence. . . . It's even that much more important as business becomes more remote, as we're operating in different continents."

—Dennis Kozlowski, CEO, Tyco International

Despite Tyco CEO Dennis Kozlowski's astute observations, not all companies are so shrewd when it comes to assessing the corporate world beyond their own limited borders. In fact, a great many companies view their surroundings in much the way most people viewed the world prior to the middle of the sixteenth century. The unshakable belief at the time was that the sun, and the rest of the universe, revolved around the Earth. With the publication of *De Revolutionibus*, Copernicus changed our understanding of the universe, forcing us to look outward. Today's corporate leaders—though successful, accomplished people—often operate as if the universe revolves around their companies.

As a result of this corporate-centric view of the universe, many companies that do an excellent job of continually examining their own operations and market achievements don't do nearly as good a job of focusing on what the competition is up to, much less on companies in other industries: what strategies they are pursuing; what management innovations they are introducing; and, especially as it relates to succession planning, what human capital infrastructure is driving them.

The danger in this myopia is that companies will remain so focused on their own systems that they will have little against which to measure just how effectively they are actually performing. In addition, they may lose sight of innovative developments elsewhere. The world may pass them by. That is why it is crucial to keep a window on the world.

All of these issues fall within the umbrella term we refer to as "global intelligence®," which we discuss extensively in this chapter. Global intelligence,® another best practice of succession planning, is best summed up as maintaining a constant awareness of management resources both inside and outside one's own company so that, in the event of a merger, CEO retirement, or other top-executive vacancy, the company is always ready with a range of options and constantly up to speed regarding its position, at all levels of the organization, compared to competitors.

The Case for Global Intelligence®

In a business environment that is infinitely more complex than ever before, many companies are finding it critical to take a broader view of the succession process. Increasingly, that includes evaluating talent both inside and outside the company. Such a comprehensive examination is critical to a successful hiring process, even if the successor will more than likely be an insider. Examining the practices of the rest of the corporate world—and the level of executive talent that is available—is important for several reasons:

• While outstanding succession candidates may appear to exist inside the company, without a frame of reference it is difficult to determine just how capable they are and whether they meet the company's changing needs.

- A well-managed, profitable company may have simply grown so rapidly or shifted its strategic focus so dramatically that no insider is immediately equipped to take over from the current CEO.

- Owner/founder companies may require a different approach to succession.

- The growing volume of mergers creates a new urgency to undertake a careful assessment of managers of both companies, starting before a corporate marriage is contemplated, to integrate the leadership development and succession planning of the newly merged company. In fact, such a human capital audit prior to a proposed merger could alert companies to potential failures because of cultural incompatibility. Mergers are the wild card in succession planning, and their anticipated impact on leadership development must be carefully examined before shuffling the management deck.

- Boards operate more than ever before in the glare of the public spotlight—with their every move creating the potential for criticism by dissident shareholder groups and the press. Directors must be able to demonstrate best efforts and due diligence. This is particularly true in the case of succession, because it is well known what a critical variable the CEO can be in company performance and stock price.

Linking Human Capital with Business Strategies

To the extent that companies scrutinize competitors, it tends to be conducted at a rather superficial level—sales and revenue figures, earnings per share—based on information easily pulled off the Internet. These are facts, which should not be confused with intelligence. They lack any judgmental or qualitative element, essentially providing merely a snapshot of where a company is at a particular point in

time, not how it has gotten there and which people are driving it. Of
course, the latter kind of information is more subtle and harder to
obtain, but it is also infinitely more useful. It can help chart a future
course for an organization and determine which leaders will guide it
along the path.

CEOs and boards require reliable intelligence on who is driving
the best businesses: the skills, styles, and personalities of people in
competitive organizations. For all the processes and strategies
employed to develop people, products, and markets, this is the missing piece of the puzzle. The lack of such global intelligence® is a huge
hole, and it is as relevant to CEO succession as it is to any other issue
related to business strategy.

As a practical matter, how could such intelligence be put to use?
Consider, for example, a company that has become interested in
"continuous improvement"—something the board and the CEO
have determined will be important in moving forward. It would
make a great deal of sense, before appointing a new CEO, to look
within those companies that have successfully implemented continuous improvement programs, or similar programs such as GE's Six
Sigma, or zero defects, two highly regarded corporate approaches to
constant improvement. It would be valuable to determine who is
responsible for these successes.

Once a company has identified the executives who have successfully devised and managed such programs in other firms, it can
benchmark its own two or three top executives against them, pairing
executives of comparable responsibility in various strategic areas. By
thinking of "intelligence gathering" in these terms, a company in the
consumer service business, for example, would be looking at executives who have introduced breakthroughs in customer service, either
through new technology or new systems, and compare how its own
team measures up. And those comparisons need not be made only
with direct competitors. The goal is to determine where the greatest
advances are being made, how, and by whom.

It is important to keep in mind that the process also requires a
company to compare its own people to others in areas it has identi-

fied for strategic emphasis. Put slightly differently, it is a process of linking human capital with business strategies.

After such an exercise, a company should be able to determine not only if it is en route to achieving its strategic goals, but also if the executive team currently on board will be able to get it there. If not, it may well be that the only way a company can reach its objectives is by pulling into its organization top performers from the best companies in the targeted strategic area. This process has as much to do with business unit succession as it does with CEO succession; the same principles apply.

A window on the world with a slightly different view can be obtained by regularly studying the practices of those companies recognized as among the all-around best-managed in the world. It might be Procter & Gamble, Coca-Cola, Emerson, or any of a handful of companies in the pantheon of consistently outstanding performers. A company seeking insight into the GE process, for example, could call upon the services of a consultant who has in-depth knowledge of what makes GE a great enterprise and what practices other companies might borrow and put into effect at home. Few companies have implemented global intelligence® on this level, but we believe the popularity of this approach will grow as great corporate leaders increasingly cross industry boundaries. From our point of view, many companies are coming to the realization that a great leader is a great leader regardless of the industry. And great leadership is infinitely more difficult to teach than industry knowledge.

Replacing the Entrepreneur/Founder

We have already discussed how global intelligence® can provide key input for important management decisions by informing CEOs and boards about key leaders both within and outside their industry as part of an ongoing benchmarking strategy linking human capital with business strategy. Global intelligence® can also play a significant role in succession planning when a company is unsure that a successor to the CEO will be found within its own ranks. This is precisely the case with Ameritrade Holding Corp., a leading Internet discount brokerage firm.

Though he is only fifty-seven years old, J. Joe Ricketts—CEO and founder of Ameritrade Holding Corp.—is in the midst of seriously planning for his successor, and global intelligence® is providing key input to the process. Ricketts explains his preoccupation by saying, "As an entrepreneurial company, we probably approach succession planning differently than many other companies." Our discussion with Ricketts illuminates some of the challenges he faces as he plans for a successor. Subsequent to our conversation, Ameritrade named Thomas Lewis Jr., who had been president of TenFold Insurance Group, co-CEO with Ricketts.

Few companies like his, says Ricketts, are able to make a smooth transition from owner/founder to professionally developed leadership. "It's very difficult. They either sell the company, or the founder of the company stays in that position too long and he is not able to take advantage of the growth in the marketplace because of capital restraints or lack of executive talent. I'm well aware of that here.

"One thing that makes our company different from most is that we're in a 'disruptive technology,' which makes it very difficult to capture the skill set you need in a leader because it's hard to gauge what the future will look like. It's all changing so rapidly. We're pioneering the Internet, and what that's doing is changing the paradigm, changing the way the financial services industry is structured. According to the Gildner Report, a leading publication that reports on our industry, 'companies pioneering disruptive technologies in new markets achieve a success rate six times higher and revenues twenty times greater than companies trying to enter established markets, even with superb technologies. Boldness and creative, out-of-the-box and off-of-the-wall thinking trump market research nearly every time. If the market already exists to research, you are too late. The surveys and focus groups are worthless.'

"Now, we're using the Internet to allow customers to gather information with which to make decisions about their financial management, and then buy and sell securities. It's having a profound impact on the securities and the financial service industries."

Ricketts' situation—making the transition from the owner/ founder of an entrepreneurial enterprise—is notoriously difficult, particularly with the added wrinkle of "disruptive technology," where change may take place so rapidly and unpredictably that it is very difficult to look ahead and discern the sorts of strategic challenges the company will be facing and thus the sort of skills and experience the company will need in the next CEO.

While in most companies Ricketts would barely be considered as within the retirement zone, he clearly feels some urgency to identify who his successor will be. Since he does not believe, because of the way the company has evolved, that the next leader will necessarily emerge from his current management team, a key part of the process is a scan of the world outside his company after some key criteria are applied.

"We're a public company, but my wife and I are still in the major stockholder position. We understand the long-term impact that the Internet is going to have on our business and we have had a wonderful success rate and nice profits and I would like to pass it to our children. We use a counseling group for family-owned businesses at Loyola University in Chicago, and one of the first things they told us is that you should have a definite plan with points in time where transfer of control will take place. You are going to fail if you merely say, 'Someday this will all be yours,' and don't have a definite plan.

"So I have told my board and family that I will not be chairman after age sixty-five; right now I am chairman and CEO. And I probably should relinquish the CEO position at the latest at age sixty-two. Now, that is kind of a scary thought for a person like myself, who is used to being in control. At the current time, I have started the process of looking and preparing for a CEO replacement by putting a corporate structure in place that we're going to have ten years from now. I'm working with our board of directors, along with an outside consultant, to help us through this evolutionary and stressful process."

Ricketts and his board are determined to do a thorough job of identifying potential successors both inside and outside the company, and the outside consulting team plays an important role. "Their job is to help us through the process of change by evaluating our executives as far as their potential for future leadership and to put a framework around the type of person who would be taking over as CEO. Ideally, we would like someone familiar with the Internet, the technology know-how, and the discount brokerage experience."

"I think that for shareholders we have to find the best person, and that person may or may not be inside. In the past as we hired people, we've never really concentrated on trying to hire somebody who would become CEO. But over the last year and a half as we have sought people for executive positions one of the criteria we have had in mind is that we want this candidate to be CEO material, to have the opportunity to compete for the CEO position."

So Ricketts is not only trying to prepare Ameritrade for his own retirement only a few years down the road, he is also helping the company make the transition from the organization he founded and presided over for many years to a much more complex, sophisticated, and professional organization. "The same talent and skills that allow an entrepreneur to get started with scarce resources and few employees are much, much different than the talent and skills that are necessary to manage a company with larger volume, a larger number of employees, and a larger customer base."

Ricketts has a clear idea of the sort of company Ameritrade will need to become to remain a leading discount brokerage firm making full use of the Internet and other cutting-edge technology, and he is using the global intelligence® model as a way of achieving this goal more rapidly. Given unlimited time, Ricketts would be able to train and develop his own future management team from within. In an environment where the technology and product offerings are likely to change dramatically within even a brief period, however, this CEO is ready to supplement gaps in leadership with outsiders to ensure that the company doesn't fall behind competitors while waiting for next-generation leaders to acquire adequate skills and experience.

GTE: Assessing Gaps and Merger Targets

Though in a very different industry and at a different stage of development than Ameritrade, telecommunications giant GTE also uses global intelligence® to keep a careful watch on emerging leaders outside the company.

According to J. Randall MacDonald, senior vice president, human resources and administration at GTE, "global intelligence® is an important piece of our succession planning process, which we call leadership development. We would much prefer to grow leaders internally because they get a sense of culture, they get a sense of nomenclature, and they get a sense of how things get done. Therefore, on the learning curve, bringing someone in from the outside means much more time and effort to bring them up to speed. That is the upside of internal development.

"We recognize, however, that we sometimes have to go outside to find the best person to fill a particular position. In order to truly protect shareholder value we have a responsibility to perform that diligence when it comes to hiring and promoting executives. Part of the process is to acknowledge that we will, from time to time, have gaps or deficiencies that need to be filled and that it may take months to accomplish this. Our view of it is to get ahead of the power curve, identify in the succession planning exercise where there may be weaknesses or gaps, then go out and identify people who may be available to us. In the event that the gap needs to be dealt with internally—because someone has been terminated or resigned—within thirty to sixty days we can put a very senior leader in there and be ready to go. I generally will earmark between five and eight positions a year where I may have gaps.

"I then rely on our search firm to tell me what is out there to fill those gaps. There may, in fact, be a dearth of people with those particular skills, which gives me the heads-up I need to develop those people internally. It's an evergreen process. We're literally recycling it all the time. It is a monthly process that culminates every March at our meeting with the board. We take four to six hours to go through our succession plans with them and give them some sense of gap analysis."

GTE uses global intelligence® somewhat differently, but just as religiously, in merger situations. Intelligence is gathered primarily though a process called third-party sourcing, wherein individuals who have worked closely with senior managers in a target company are tapped for their views on the skills, abilities, and personalities of these individuals. MacDonald says, "We believe global intelligence® is a crucial exercise when we are in the process of acquiring or merging with a company; it is essential for us to understand the quality of the leadership in that company. Not only are you buying the physical assets, the financial assets, but more importantly, you are buying leadership. You are taking your shareholders' money and investing it in a new company. You want to have some level of assurance that the quality of the leadership required to achieve your goals is there. If it isn't there, you'd better know that going in, so that you can react to it and put the right kind of leaders in up front. In this way, you don't come to realize that something you bought was broken because you didn't have high-quality leadership.

"The analogy that is often made is that it's due diligence on the human capital side, and I don't think people often think about it in that way. People usually only associate due diligence with assessing the financial side of the proposed deal. Most people who pick up the *Wall Street Journal* believe that corporations buy other corporations to make money, which is true. But you are also buying the people, and you have to determine ahead of time precisely what you are getting. That's one thing we have been consistent about in the last two to three years. We recognize that you can go out and buy the best business in the world, but if you don't have the right leaders running it, it's going to go in the tank and ultimately your shareholders are going to pay."

This is how GTE uses global intelligence® as a best practice. Regardless of the specific circumstances—whether a company is considering merging with another one or benchmarking its own talent—decision-makers have to have a broad-based, objective, and systematic way of assessing the human talent that is involved.

Corporate Cultures: Tricky to Merge

As Randy MacDonald alluded to, the challenge of merging two cultures—including two often very distinct styles of management, management development, and succession planning—should not be underestimated. It is no wonder that, since these deals have traditionally been driven by investment bankers, the focus has been chiefly on the financial fit of the proposed partners. In recent years, however, as mergers have increased in frequency and scale, mismatches are ever more costly and disruptive, internally as well as to shareholders. That is why companies considering such a step are increasingly focusing on a rigorous assessment prior to any deal to ascertain whether two companies will likely be compatible.

This sort of assessment is particularly crucial in the context of succession planning, because a merger is likely to change all the rules a company may have previously observed in the realm of leadership development, training, and grooming executives for various positions. Companies that might serve as textbook examples of best practices when it comes to succession planning will find that their laudable efforts to develop management talent and carefully position successors at all levels of the organization may mean little when succession suddenly involves planning for not one but two different organizations.

Nineteen ninety-eight was certainly a banner year for the announcement of corporate engagements. At the end of November alone, ten major corporate mergers were announced, most notably the union of America Online and Netscape as well as Exxon and Mobil. While there is typically much excitement generated in the media and markets about such prospective combinations, it is not at all unusual to see them fall apart only a few months down the road. The reason? Long-term compatibility is not defined by the numbers and business strategy but by the people who make the numbers and carry out the business strategy. And if there is no way of effectively meshing two corporate cultures, a merger will not work, no matter how good it may look on paper. Consider these high-profile examples:

- Announced in June 1998, the merger between American Home Products (AHP) and Monsanto was called off only a few months later. Despite the potential advantages of creating research efficiencies and a bigger pool of scientific talent, it became clear that trying to merge a frugal, rigidly run company like AHP with a high-spending, risk-taking one like Monsanto would not be an easy fit. Differences reportedly ranged from who should be assigned to corporate headquarters to how much top executives should be paid. The mismatch was a costly one: When the deal was canceled, Monsanto's shares lost 27 percent of their value, and AHP's fell 10 percent.

• AT&T had a similar experience when it took over NCR in the early 1990s, but discovered the problems only after it was too late. AT&T's unionized employees objected to working in the same building as NCR's nonunion staff. NCR's conservative, centralized management culture was turned inside out by AT&T's insistence on calling supervisors "coaches" and removing executives' office doors. Those who had initially made NCR profitable left in droves, so that by 1997 only four of the top thirty NCR managers at the time of the takeover still worked for the company. By the time AT&T finally spun off NCR, the failure of the deal had cost AT&T more than $3 billion and NCR about half its market value.

• In 1996, when Wells Fargo took the lead in a bidding war for First Interstate, many top executives from the target company jumped ship before the takeover was even consummated. Once the deal was completed, the new bank became victim of a clash between Wells Fargo's emphasis on high-tech banking and First Interstate's long-standing commitment to personal service. The loss of First Interstate's people who knew how to keep customers happy contributed to an 11.8 percent decline in deposits over the course of fifteen months. Wells Fargo, once the most profitable bank in the country, saw its stock rise at half the rate of the S&P major index for banks, and was exposed to the risk of being taken over itself.

Without expending much effort, one could quickly unearth many other examples where little effort was made to determine in terms of common sense and practicality—not merely dollars and cents—

whether certain mergers should be pursued. The purpose of high-lighting such mismatches and their impact on the companies' stock value is not merely to frighten, but also to enlighten. As we have discussed extensively, particularly in chapter 4 ("Looking Deep Within the Organization"), succession planning, if it is done properly, involves far more than merely the veneer of leadership at the top of the organization. It also means planning for leadership and succession at every level so that companies can develop their own talent, from the bottom up.

Since mergers often make years of this kind of careful, thoughtful development irrelevant, it only makes sense to rigorously anticipate and analyze what sort of structure will be taking its place. How will the management culture of the anticipated partner mesh with your own? What will the management structure of the new entity look like? Is there likely to be a loss of valued talent? These are all questions companies will want to seriously consider—and here's the important part—*before* the merger is announced on the front page of the *Wall Street Journal*.

Gauging Compatibility

We have long been leading advocates of performing extensive human capital audits—in addition to the traditional financial due diligence—prior to serious and public consideration of a merger.

It is easy, however, to be swept up in the excitement of the deal—of the anticipated synergies and efficiencies—as the former co-CEO of Cigna Corporation, Ralph Saul, so eloquently expresses in chapter 9. Amid all the premerger headiness, however, it is critical that the board and the CEO be as convinced of the cultural fit of the two companies as they are of the strategic and financial fit. Unfortunately, many CEOs who need to carefully evaluate whether a deal is indeed "doable" rely on investment bankers for not only the financial assessment but also for the assessment on how well the management of the two organizations will be able to work together in achieving objectives outlined in the deal. In our view, there is clearly a conflict in representing both sides of this equation. Even if there is no intent to mislead a client, we do not believe that investment bankers, who are focused on the numbers and getting the deal done, can adequately and objectively assess the human capital side.

We strongly recommend that companies hire an independent third party to evaluate the management of any company they are seriously considering acquiring or merging with. Further, the results of such an analysis should be as rigorous as a financial analysis and should carry equal weight when determining whether to proceed with the transaction. Such studies typically focus on top executives, usually direct reports to the CEO, and divisional executives, when appropriate. Assessments should do far more than scratch the surface and should provide in-depth biographical information as well as an analysis of professional strengths and weaknesses, style, character, values, and general reputation of targeted individuals and management teams. As a result, clients will derive key strategic information about executive talent that impacts valuation, business plans, and the ability to move quickly in staffing top positions at the close of a deal.

Financial analysts and investment bankers rarely acquire this sort of information because they are unlikely to interview senior executives in a specific field or alumni of a corporation, who can often tell far more about a company than a decade's worth of balance books can. These are the people who can and will provide the answers to tough questions about the target company: Will the right people come together to make decisions and create results? How long do the top executives intend to stay? Are employees promoted on tenure or on talent? Do ideas "not made here" stand a chance of survival through corporate review? Are there powerful players who will impede change?

This sort of probing is the most reliable way to ascertain, from a critical people perspective, whether a deal is sound and should be undertaken. Whether this assessment puts a seal of approval on the deal, which is often the case, or nixes it altogether, it helps companies bolster the decision-making process with specific, concrete evidence to support a conclusion of why a merger will or will not work. This approach is surely preferable to proceeding merely on the basis of financial analyses and keeping one's fingers crossed that any issues with management teams will simply sort themselves out.

Only after the CEO and the board have the opportunity to view all supporting evidence and determine that both the financial and human capital sides of the deal look solid, should they proceed. But even after the deal is undertaken and the investment bankers move on to their next transaction, the company will only have completed phase one of its management analysis. In the context of a merger or acquisition, crucial goals related to management teams of the respective companies should be viewed as follows:

- *Phase one, as we've discussed, is the premerger and acquisition due diligence phase.* At this stage companies need to do their homework to determine whether they have the right executives to do the deal and who will occupy key positions at the close of the deal. No less important is phase two.

- *Phase two, the postmerger and acquisition integration phase.* At this stage, companies will need to further evaluate their management resources with an eye toward more permanent staffing decisions that will best integrate the optimal resources they have in both organizations.

As a firm that regularly works with a number of clients to resolve all of these management challenges related to merging with or acquiring another company, we cannot overstate the importance, in both the pre- and post-transaction phases, of relying on a process that is viewed by all parties as thorough and objective. By focusing on methodology and process rather than relationships and politics, companies not only help to ensure a rigorous evaluation of executives' skills, performance, and potential, they also promote an atmosphere of fairness and a perception that success will be based on ability and merit. And setting the right tone going forward may greatly influence the ability of the organization to hold on to management talent as well as the overall performance of the enterprise.

Lest we forget how this discussion of global intelligence®, human capital, and mergers relates to succession, allow us to loop back for just a moment to reinforce the following logical progression:

- Succession is an ongoing process.

- Succession should properly be viewed in the larger context of management development at all levels throughout the company, not merely as a change at the top.

- Companies that are truly adept at management development and succession will have a continual, self-renewing succession culture, with leaders emerging from the bottom up.

- Because mergers, by definition, entail management redundancies and require integration, the best-laid management development and succession plans will likely be disrupted.

- A primary focus of CEOs and boards prior to and following mergers and acquisitions must be how they can not only integrate and unify management but also build back in solid management development and succession planning.

As company examples such as GTE and Ameritrade highlight, some of the best-managed companies have integrated a global intelligence® perspective into their succession planning efforts. Even those companies with a primary focus on developing talent internally know that they can easily become too insular and lose their edge if they lose sight of the leaders whom competitors and other world-class companies are developing. In the case of mergers, of course, the input of global intelligence® is critical to getting over some major hurdles, including whether, from a management/cultural viewpoint, the deal should be done in the first place, and, if it is, how management teams can best be integrated and succession put firmly back on track.

Board Checklist

How can boards ensure that their companies use global intelligence® effectively, and provide themselves with a window on the world? Our board checklist for chapter 8 stresses some of the priorities companies should keep in mind when using this tool:

1. Consider implementing—as an integral part of the management development process—a systematic way to regularly benchmark in-house management talent against competitors within your industry as well as leading companies worldwide. In addition to assessing top executives, such a process will yield valuable intelligence on best practices, alternate structures, and compensation trends.

2. Link business strategy with human capital infrastructure—that is, carefully consider the strategic goals of the organization, then identify the executives who will enable you to achieve them.

3. In annual management reviews with the CEO, focus on potential gaps in the management team and what is being done to address possible deficits internally and, if required, externally.

4. Prior to serious consideration of a merger, discuss with the CEO the importance of undertaking a human capital audit, the management equivalent of financial due diligence. Such an analysis should carefully assess the skills and abilities of a target's executive team and bring into relief any potential culture conflicts between the two organizations.

5. Equally important as the premerger human capital audit is the postmerger integration of management resources. Consider a third-party assessment of management to provide needed input into staffing decisions to ensure a rigorous process and one that is perceived as fair to all participants.

Clearly, the recent wave of mergers has brought with it new issues of concern for boards. Some we have discussed in this chapter. Another issue, the increased popularity of co-CEOs—sometimes a consequence of mergers of equals—is one we discuss in chapter 9, "Flashing Yellow Light: Potential Problems Ahead." The co-CEO relationship is not the only situation where boards are advised to proceed with caution. In the same chapter we also advise boards on other potentially difficult succession scenarios, including when a director becomes CEO and when an ex-CEO remains on the board. The final challenge in chapter 9: cultivating a relationship with the media when it comes to succession that goes beyond "no comment" to maintaining an ongoing dialogue.

9

Flashing Yellow Light:
Potential Problems Ahead

We have consistently focused on best practices that leading companies implement to ensure effective succession planning. But as the seventeenth-century Japanese writer Ihara Saikaku noted: "There is always something to upset the most careful of human calculations."

We'd like to depart from our best-practices format to address some practices that, while not uncommon, are not necessarily recommended. Depending on the circumstances at a particular company at a given time, however, they may represent the best alternative available. Whatever the situation, it is advisable for boards and CEOs to choose a particular route with eyes wide open, aware of the pitfalls inherent in their choice.

Quite often the greatest pressures to depart from established best practices result from relatively new corporate trends, with which boards may find themselves face-to-face, including:

- an unprecedented number of mergers, which, among other effects, create pressures to appoint co-CEOs;

- the growing influence of institutional investors, many of whom are seeking a major role in the succession process;

• closer scrutiny by the news media, which can derail a succession process if a board is not sufficiently prepared.

In addition to these newer challenges, boards must tread carefully in dealing with potentially dicey scenarios that emerge from time to time, including hiring a director as CEO, and maintaining a departed CEO on the board.

This chapter provides guidance for boards on how to deal with a range of these departure-from-the-norm practices. We've put a "flashing yellow light" before these practices, not because they should never be used, but so boards can recognize the possible dangers in using them and can carefully and judiciously assess when and how they should be used.

When and How Co-CEOs Are Most Effective

Ihara Saikaku's warning is particularly relevant in our merger-manic age. Indeed, companies that have focused for years on leadership development and carefully planned succession may suddenly find all their planning is for naught if they enter into a "merger of equals" where they must find a way to mesh two cultures that may be vastly different from each other. Even boards that have been very involved in succession planning may find themselves sitting idly by as their plans are wrecked in the wake of the merger. Of course, it is also possible that the same merger may provide a successor, just in the nick of time, for a CEO who has not yet provided for a one, coming to the rescue of a board that has been negligent in fulfilling its succession-planning responsibilities.

The not-infrequent outcome of a merger—when it is indeed a merger of equals—is a co-CEO arrangement for an indefinite or sometimes a defined period. This arrangement has become increasingly common, garnering much speculation among the press on how someone bred to be the boss can "cohabitate" at the top with another, equally strong, CEO.

More than sixteen years ago, however, when INA Corporation and Connecticut General, two large insurance holding companies, merged, such a power-sharing relationship was much more of an anomaly. Ralph Saul, who had led INA and represented half of the leadership of the merged entity, Cigna Corporation, has had a good deal of time to reflect on the nature of the co-CEO relationship, what makes it work or not work, and the impact and implications for succession planning. His experience, combined with a decade and a half of hindsight, may be of interest to the CEOs and boards of those companies that have only recently attempted power sharing at the top of their companies.

After INA merged with Connecticut General, says Saul, "I served as chairman and my colleague, Robert Kilpatrick, as president, with both of us as co-chiefs. This arrangement was unusual at the time, and it raised many questions with the financial community and the press. Our merger, after many frustrating years, ultimately fulfilled the strategic objectives we had set for Cigna. However, in the course of the merger, our boards learned a great deal about power sharing between chief executives and the enormous difficulties in merging two large companies."

Saul finds it surprising that boards that may previously have played an active role in succession planning may be willing to sit back when all the careful planning goes out the window as a result of a merger.

"It's amazing. For heaven's sake, here you have a board that has invested all this time in succession planning. They have their yearly meeting with the CEO, in which the CEO goes through a succession plan. They discuss, with some frequency, the range of possible successors within the company. And then, as time goes on, the CEO says, 'Look, I've narrowed it down to two candidates.' He then gets feedback from his human resources or organizational committee. Then finally comes the time where he says, 'This is the guy who should succeed me.' There are many companies where this is done according to a very orderly process. You know the companies, Procter & Gamble, and so on, where there is a religion built around the selection of the CEO. But then you do a merger as equals. These two guys, these two CEOs, sit down and say, 'We're going to share power,' or have an arrangement where one succeeds the other. What's amazing and ironic is that after all this succession planning, here these two guys make the decision for the board. Obviously, the board can change it, but what I'm getting at, particularly if there's a co-CEO structure, is that they've changed the whole succession plan and the dynamics of the succession. The co-CEOs take away, at least temporarily, something that the board has regarded as its divine prerogative."

The CEOs of the respective companies involved in making the deal, says Saul, rely on the investment bankers for their management advice, which is part of the problem. "Investment bankers have become much more sophisticated in this area—in how to get these co-CEOs together, and how to work something out that might be acceptable to both of them. Investment bankers have displaced boards in a way because the board doesn't go out to talk to management consultants at that point in a merger. Obviously, the discussions about the mergers of equals is highly confidential so the only ones involved are boards and the investment bankers acting as management consultants. The investment bankers, of course, have a strong interest in getting the deal done. It's quite a conflict."

Saul is an advocate of boards remaining involved throughout merger discussions, rather than relinquishing their responsibilities to outsiders, such as investment bankers, who may be less than objective regarding leadership decisions. It is critical that boards know the right questions to ask, and when it comes to mergers and the impact on succession planning, boards need to get satisfactory answers to questions about the structure of the top job and succession before approving a merger.

According to Saul, "an initial question for boards to ask should be, Why have the chief executives agreed to a power-sharing agreement? Is it to get the deal done, or is it a permanent arrangement that the chief executives honestly believe makes sense for managing the merged company?

"We started out merger discussions because the business of our two companies complemented one another and we saw the potential for enormous cost savings through the consolidation of overlapping operations. As chief executives, we shared a common vision of where our businesses were going in the changing environment for health care delivery and in the insurance markets. Despite the strategic fit between our two companies, only a power-sharing arrangement would get the deal done. Neither company wished to be acquired, and neither of us was willing to give up the role of chief executive officer. There were other reasons for the structure—to facilitate the merger, to ensure that the interests of our employees and hometown communities were represented, and to avoid paying a premium. While these reasons were important, the fact was that ego and ambition primarily drove our decision."

INA's board did in fact play an important role, premerger, by engaging Saul in discussion about the proposed co-CEO arrangement and pressing for answers that would put the board at ease with what it considered a potentially difficult relationship. "One of our wiser board members called me before the merger was presented to our board for approval and warned that, while he would vote for the merger, I would be embarking on the most difficult and painful management exercise in my business career. In the business world, he observed, there are no marriages made in heaven. How right he was! In the end, our board was assured by my desire to terminate the co-CEO structure by retiring within two years and by the business sense of the merger."

During premerger discussions with his board, Saul says one of his directors pressed him on the possibility of corporate clashes because of the vastly different organizations that would be merging: Connecticut General, more hierarchical and control-oriented, as opposed to the more entrepreneurial INA. While she asked Saul to contemplate these possible roadblocks, Saul admits that such issues were set aside in the excitement of the merger. "Like most chief executives," he says, "consumed by the strategic fit of the companies and the growth possibilities that lay ahead, the abstract notion of culture clashes seemed manageable.

"After consummation of the merger, when premerger euphoria had worn off and the hard work began, however," remembers Saul, "our differences began to emerge. These differences centered on issues such as the pace of consolidating common businesses and reducing staff; the selection of the managers for some of our businesses; relationships with the board; and the site of the permanent headquarters for the company. Within one year after the merger, I decided to resign as chief executive officer but remain as chairman. Since Bob would eventually have sole responsibility for managing the company, it made sense for him to make these decisions. While difficult to accept, I concluded there was no way to make our power-sharing arrangement work and, in the interests of the new company, it made sense for me to step aside. Our differences in personality and style were just too great."

Co-CEOs with a Built-in Succession Plan

If all goes as planned in the fourth quarter of 1999, GTE and Bell Atlantic will be entering into a partnership—also a merger of equals—and the respective CEOs, Charles Lee of GTE and Ivan Seidenberg, who recently succeeded Ray Smith at Bell Atlantic, have already begun to work together as a team.

Mergers of equals and co-CEO relationships are far more common today than back sixteen years ago when Cigna was formed from the merger of INA and Connecticut General. While there is now more of a track record for these transactions and relationships, it is clear that the headiness of the proposed deal and the push from those on the financial side may still override serious consideration of the softer, cultural side and equal assessment of the wisdom and anticipated success of merging two particular companies. Only recently have companies begun to give sufficient weight to the cultural factors that may sabotage a merger whose numbers looked so impressive.

Lee, Seidenberg, and their respective boards have spent a great deal of time discussing how best to mesh the two cultures, according to Lee, probably as much time or more as was spent scrutinizing the financial side of the merger. According to Lee, the GTE board has worked closely with him analyzing all aspects of the merger each step of the way.

"They were deeply, totally, and thoroughly involved in being satisfied that the merger is the right thing to do. In a merger of equals, you don't have premiums. Acquisitions are a big challenge for the board of directors because they have to consider if the company is worth the premium they have to pay. In this case there's no premium, so they didn't have that to wrestle with that.

"Most of the conversation with the board was about the meshing of the cultures, the meshing of the people, and executive succession. Succession had to be done differently from what we've been accustomed to because we're two diffe`rent organizations coming together. We have, however, put together a succession plan for the next five to seven years. I will be chairman and co-CEO until I retire on June 30, 2002, and Ivan will be co-CEO and president. After I retire, I become nonexecutive chairman for two more years, and Ivan is the sole CEO. When I leave in 2004, Ivan becomes chairman and CEO. Particularly given Ivan's personality, skills, and talents, I think that's a wonderful succession plan and one that our board of directors has endorsed."

Both CEOs and their boards are already thinking far beyond Seidenberg's tenure as CEO. Given the commitment both companies have long had to succession and leadership development, it is not surprising that they remain focused on these in the midst of plans for the merger. They are carefully recalibrating their leadership development process to serve the new combined entity. "We are already planning for who will succeed Ivan and how we will have a leadership development process for the new company that will bring forward people five to ten years younger who are in a position to replace him way down the road. Management and CEO succession is something we have spent a lot of time planning for in this merger of equals."

Shifting gears from one company to two combined companies consumed a great deal of the CEOs' and the boards' time. Working out the relationship between the two co-CEOs was not nearly as difficult. "I don't think the issue of sharing power, or 'cohabitating,' as it is often referred to, is as difficult or complicated as it is made out to be. I feel totally comfortable, as does our board and the Bell Atlantic board. Of course, what works for us wouldn't necessarily work for anyone else; every organization is different."

Mergers aside, Lee also sees power sharing as the way of the future, especially in a fast-moving, innovative industry. "Partnerships in today's world—sharing power, teamwork, employee involvement, coming up with the best solution, respecting your coworkers—is clearly far more important when technology is changing so rapidly, and I'm talking about at every level of the corporation. Ivan and I have far different backgrounds and are different ages. He came up through AT&T starting as a line splicer working at Bell, but he was all over AT&T before the divestiture and then at Nynex he had a whole series of jobs, including in the Washington office. My background has been financial planning throughout the whole history of my career until I became president of this company. We have complementary backgrounds."

Ultimately, Lee views power sharing as a positive phenomenon, though he believes the media often choose to focus on only the negative aspects. "It's not clear to me that in all cases these arrangements are forced upon the people—which seems to be the common perception—in order to make a deal work. It may be, in fact, that it is the best approach and the best model for a combination like a Travellers and a Citicorp or between a Bell Atlantic and GTE. These are big companies with lots of people and different cultures, and in fact a meshing or a blending of the cultures is a high-priority job in launching the new company. Having shared power and responsibility, and real teamwork at the leadership level, one can argue, would greatly enhance the accomplishment of that goal and objective."

There are other, concrete benefits that should accrue to shareholders, according to Lee, in the GTE–Bell Atlantic merger going forward. "The whole design that Ivan and I envision is truly a combination of equals—a sharing, a blending. We both think that's absolutely essential. Both shareholder groups will benefit from the accomplishment of the teams rather than one group getting a head start and the other having to catch up and pay that premium off before they benefit. These power-sharing arrangements come in all shapes and forms. What we have in our particular combination is not only a merger of equals, a meshing of two cultures, but a succession plan. It was clear to me that Ivan is an extremely capable and talented person. The Bell

Atlantic board apparently thought so because they made him chairman and CEO. While our board of directors may not yet know Ivan as well, from a distance they can see that Ivan is the kind of person who is the leader of the future for this combined enterprise."

A Word of Caution About Merger Motives

In the mergers we have just discussed, the CEOs made it clear—and there is certainly ample evidence to support their views—that the mergers were undertaken for sound business reasons. In some cases, however, the motives of the CEO initiating the merger may be more suspect. It is the job of the board to pass on the appropriateness of the deal. Unless it makes solid business sense, it should never be undertaken primarily to provide a successor for a CEO who has not prepared properly or so a CEO can go out in a blaze of glory.

It is critical that the board determine what human factors are behind management's recommendation to pursue a merger strategy. On a related subject, we did an analysis a few years ago of twenty-four spin-offs during a three-year period, and found that two-thirds had been initiated by CEOs in the "retirement zone," meaning they were age fifty-eight or older.

One might wonder whether the outcome of our study might have been vastly different had these executives been at the peak of their careers, when they might have been more concerned about the long term. We have also heard reports that CEOs may use spin-offs to reward or get rid of top executives who want to replace them, and, further, as a way to spin off corporate directors to new entities.

One has to be careful, though, not to paint with too broad a brush. Many mergers that are undertaken for sound business reasons also provide a well-equipped long-term successor for a CEO who will be stepping down and for the combined entity. The point is that it is the board's responsibility to ask the right questions of the CEO regarding the merger strategy, and then to determine whether it is in the company's long-term interests to proceed.

The Long Good-bye:
When the Ex-CEO Remains on Board

Though it does indeed seem to work well for some companies, we would not recommend as a best practice that the retiring CEO remain on the board. While a relatively common practice, it is not necessarily a prescription for success and, like the co-CEO relationship, it is one that should be approached with caution. Jack Welch, when queried on the subject of any continued involvement with GE's board, has indicated that when he retires, he is "out of there" totally and completely. CEOs who are reputed to be tough, outspoken, and independent often seem surprisingly intuitive about bowing out and cutting off ties with the board after retirement.

Robert Crandall, who had been CEO of AMR Corp. and American Airlines, Inc., since 1985, literally sailed off into the sunset when he retired and relinquished his board seat in April 1998 with plans to cross the Atlantic in his forty-nine-foot, custom-made sailboat. We spoke with Crandall just days before he left the company, and he expressed strong views about the CEO cutting his ties with the company and the board upon retirement.

"I firmly believe that the retiring CEO should not remain on the board," he told us. "The new management should have the ability to set its own policies without any inference that what the prior guy did was wrong. The new CEO shouldn't be burdened with the political implications of changing the predecessor's policies. For that reason I have always felt that when the CEO retires, he should simply retire. That doesn't mean he dies or drops off the planet; when you want his advice you just pick up the phone."

Asked why he thought many CEOs found it so hard to cut the ties, Crandall said, "There are very powerful established social relationships between board members and management—many of my closest friends are AMR management and board members. You don't want to sever your ties and your sense of continuity; you don't want to leave the community you've lived in for forty years; you don't want to leave your family. There's a strong social motivation to remain part of the group. The decision to leave is an intellectual decision and it flies in the face of the emotional pull you feel."

Crandall's own predecessor remained on the board after handing over the reins to him, though, as Crandall recalls, it didn't cramp his style as CEO one bit. "It didn't inhibit my behavior at all," states Crandall, renowned as a powerful, hard-charging CEO. "I made it clear that the decisions were mine and not his."

When we spoke with Ray Smith in July 1998, Bell Atlantic had just announced his retirement and the fact that he would be succeeded by Ivan Seidenberg. Like Crandall, Smith has had a reputation as strong, highly capable, and accustomed to speaking his mind. When it came to retirement, however, he, too, was prepared to make a clean break. "I don't think the departing CEO should remain on the board. When I leave employment at the end of this year, I won't remain on the board. The reasons are eminently obvious. The policies I had as CEO may no longer be operative. . . . I won't know why, I'm no longer involved in the day-to-day. . . . Suppose I said we should never get into China. The new CEO may have different views. . . . It would be hard for him to say, 'By the way, you know the notion you had about China? Well, you were dead wrong!' . . . Why hobble that person with my ten years? Why not free him immediately?"

Common Element

It is worth noting that one reason why the co-CEO relationship and the retired CEO remaining on the board are more often than not difficult to manage is the power-sharing element they have in common. On a long-term basis, these sorts of arrangements just don't seem to go down well with American CEOs. Despite all the recent emphasis on team building and empowerment at all levels in U.S. companies, this concept seems to extend only so far. Though perhaps much flattened, the organizational pyramid is alive and well, and it seems that having more than one individual in charge is a very tough balancing act indeed. This is a major reason why the splitting of the CEO and chairman roles—increasingly the rule in U.K. and other European countries—has never really taken hold in the United States. When it comes down to it, American CEOs function best when they can run their own show.

During the course of our interviews, a number of CEOs who have indicated publicly that they had no problem with their predecessor remaining on the board told us privately that, in the words of one CEO, "having the retired CEO remain on the board was a major pain in the ass for me. How could it not loom over every aspect of strategy discussion and decision making? Every time you change direction, it's like a slap in the face to the old CEO, who is still seated right across the boardroom table from you! It can't help but hamper your ability to perform as CEO, and if you are working with primarily the same board, directors may feel that their loyalties are divided. If they go along with a new initiative, are they repudiating the decisions of your predecessor? I have vowed not to put my successor in such an untenable position; when I'm gone, I'm gone."

Nearly every CEO we spoke with indicated a sensitivity to power-sharing issues and how best to resolve them. Clateo Castellini—who had been Becton, Dickinson's CEO since Raymond Gilmartin left suddenly in June 1994 to join Merck as CEO—stepped down in January 1999, but remained chairman, and was succeeded by president Edward Ludwig. Our discussion with Castellini, which took place well before the transition was announced, illustrates his sensitivity to the issue of sharing power with a successor.

"Whether or not I will remain on the board is currently a big conversation with my own board," admits Castellini. Perhaps having once been burned by the abrupt departure of the former CEO, BD is especially conscious of maintaining continuity should they ever again experience such an event. The board is not eager to lose Castellini, who has already postponed his retirement for several years to take over as CEO when Gilmartin left, and has encouraged him to remain as chairman or, at least, on the board. "I don't think it is a good thing," confides Castellini. "It would have been impossible for me to do the same job I did if Ray had remained on the board or as chairman. It is difficult because it is impossible for the old CEO not to inhibit his successor. Given my style and personality, I probably could have found a way to live with such a situation, but I sincerely believe one of the secrets of good management is to let people work with freedom. You make the best choice you can and then you let the new person fly on his own. If you give him a little freedom but retain a piece of the control, it's difficult for leaders to accomplish anything, so I don't favor that approach."

An approach that Castellini might consider is a setup where he remains "on call," but separate enough from day-to-day operations to give any successor the space he or she may need to put his or her own stamp on the company's strategy and operations. As a result of some suggestions proffered on a future transitional role after he steps down as CEO, Castellini indicates that he might be amenable to a situation where he maintains a separate office with his own secretary for a brief period—perhaps a couple of years—making himself available if the new CEO requires his participation in various events, giving a speech, for example, or in some way functioning as an elder states-man or company ambassador.

"I'm told this approach has been very successful in other compa-nies, where the retired CEO stays on as an unpaid consultant doing only those things specifically requested by the CEO. The son of the founder, Mr. Becton, functioned in a similar capacity when he retired. He was available for meetings when needed and pitched in in other ways. He was not a true manager, but he filled an important role representing the history and values of the company. Perhaps I could continue to serve the company in this way, but I wouldn't con-sider doing it without the complete endorsement of the new CEO."

Castellini acknowledges that part of the board's reluctance is related to jitters regarding any transition, although the stringent suc-cession planning process, which was beefed up after Gilmartin's departure, will likely make a transition quite smooth. He remains confident that during the period before the company shifts to another CEO, the board will become increasingly comfortable with prospective successors through increased exposure and that any apprehension by the board is likely to resolve itself.

When a Director Becomes CEO

Though the path from the boardroom to the CEO's office is not a well-worn one, it is not unheard of for a director to be appointed CEO. While there are specific instances where it can be of great value to a company to have a director capable of taking over as CEO, we caution companies to use this practice judiciously.

One scenario in which a company might want to consider having a director—assuming there is one who is qualified—take on the role of CEO temporarily might be when the CEO is ready to step down, or must leave suddenly. The company may have an excellent candidate it wishes to hold on to who is not yet ready for the responsibilities of CEO. In such a case, a director may be asked to assume the position of CEO for a specified period of perhaps two to three years, until the successor is ready.

A particularly complex example of this is Thermo Electron Corp., a $4 billion diversified company in Boston, which anointed director Richard Syron (former chairman and CEO of the American Stock Exchange) in March 1999. The board had determined that no executive in the management ranks was ready to assume the top job. Further, it would be very difficult to attract a capable outsider, given the company's unique culture and structure of twenty-three spin-outs— in reality an actively managed portfolio of companies. Succession at Thermo Electron is discussed in greater detail in chapter 3.

A twist on this scenario is when you have an incoming CEO who has never operated in a boardroom and doesn't understand the mechanics and the dynamics. It would not be a bad idea in this case to slowly transition the new CEO into the dual role of chairman and CEO, with the retiring CEO serving as nonexecutive chairman for a couple of years. If the board establishes a clear time frame for the transition, this interim arrangement can work quite well.

Examples of companies that have used this practice—of elevating a director to the CEO position—to their advantage include Eli Lilly & Company, Lucent Technologies, and Texas Instruments (which we discuss in detail in chapter 2).

These are not everyday practices, but they can be successfully implemented, and it is always good to have the talent and resources inside the company to step in when needed. For what it deems a temporary arrangement, as in the case of a younger CEO who may just need a bit more seasoning, the board may be wise not to seek an outside solution that might prompt an undesired departure. As with all of the "flashing yellow light" practices, however, the board must proceed cautiously, asking the right questions and helping to craft the most appropriate solutions.

Organizing the Board to Get the Job Done

Another way in which the succession process can easily become unhinged is if the board itself is not efficiently organized to minimize internal discord and to get the job done. We have personally witnessed successions that should have proceeded apace, but, instead, have fallen apart at the seams because the board had established no real system to deal properly with the multitude of tasks involved in identifying and evaluating succession candidates and bringing the process to a conclusion. Under the worst circumstances, the process drags on and excellent internal and external candidates become fed up and look to other opportunities, and the company's prospects for hiring a capable successor are diminished.

As we've said, there are myriad tasks the board must accomplish in the succession process, including:

- deciding on what guideposts must be met along the way;

- deciding which inside candidates to consider;

- timing and the transition with the incumbent;

- determining whether a premium will have to be paid on compensation to attract outside candidates;

- establishing selection criteria;

- deciding how issues will be resolved when the board is divided;

• deciding how many candidates will be assessed and who will assess them;

• deciding how the board will handle the issue of references vs. maintaining confidentiality.

As a firm, we have advised thousands of companies on succession-related matters, and one of the most important pieces of advice we can give to streamline the process is for the board to designate a search or selection committee and chairman who together can decide how best to deal with some of the aforementioned issues. In our opinion, smaller is clearly better; three seems to be an ideal number. As with any group decision-making effort, difficulty resolving succession issues seems to increase geometrically as each new member is added to the group. A small committee, therefore, charged with the responsibility for the entire board, works best.

This does not mean that others on the board have no voice or responsibility for succession; quite the contrary. While the search committee does much of the legwork, it is essential that others remain informed and involved and have the opportunity to add their judgment and assessment of candidates to the decision-making process. Kenneth Macke, general partner, Macke Partners, and veteran search committee chair whom we worked with on the Unisys succession when Lawrence Weinbach was appointed CEO, has some definite ideas on how boards can structure things to allow for the appropriate participation of the entire board and at the same time keep from becoming mired in unending discussions and decision making.

"The board has to take charge of the process," says Macke, "but someone has to lead that charge. Therein lies the secret to success." And who, according to Macke, should lead the charge? "Ideally, the retired CEO of a major company who has sat in the chairman's seat and has the time and flexibility to do the job right. Someone who's been on the dance floor."

Having served on three separate board CEO selection committees—Unisys, U.S. Bank Corp., and Pillsbury—Macke has some tried-and-true advice for other boards. Although the search committee may do much of the work involved, it is essential, he says, to bring the whole board into the process from the very beginning. "By keeping all involved throughout," Macke says, "everyone has the opportunity to express his or her views and they don't start coming out of the woodwork later on. There's a level of trust established between the committee and the board early on, and the committee has to maintain that trust with frequent reports to the board, keeping all fully informed." Communication is key, he says, so that there is never the appearance of secrecy. "When I have been in the role of leading a board's succession effort I have always tried to bubble up differences in front of the entire group so that all feel their concerns have been addressed and difficult issues can be resolved."

The search committee can also be instrumental in other key areas, including dealing with the press (which we discuss later in this chapter) and in ensuring that the new CEO has the help he or she needs from the board to be successful.

While Macke believes search firms are helpful, he discourages undue reliance on them, stressing that the bottom-line responsibility for both the process and the results rests with the board. "Boards have to develop candidate criteria. Search firms can tee up ideas, but the board has to make up its mind and even change its mind." He cautions boards to beware of search firms that oversell candidates and emphasizes the importance of due diligence by the board, including proper reference checking. We vigorously support this view of the role of search firms, and we explore this issue further in chapter 5.

How Big a Voice to Large Institutional Investors?

"Too many cooks. . . ." That adage may well be applied to the succession process, whether regarding the participation of board members or outsiders such as large institutional investors, who may believe it is their divine right to have a hand in the selection of the CEO. Boards may feel intimidated by the magnitude of the investors' holdings as well as their right to "vote with their feet" if they are displeased. To put it concisely, it is never wise to ignore the opinions of a major shareholder, but the board has to determine an appropriate role that encourages participation while not allowing such input to grow beyond proper boundaries that impinge on the board's ultimate responsibility for the outcome of the process.

Clearly major institutional shareholders need to be afforded the opportunity to express their views and feel that their concerns are being addressed. But while their views on the spec (selection criteria for the CEO) and candidates should be solicited, they should not be part of the actual jury that will make the ultimate decision. When we have dealt with institutional shareholders during a search, we have often been careful to get feedback from them prior to any announcement, but we feel strongly that they should not have veto power. Regardless of the board's efforts, they will vote with their feet anyway, and they should never control the selection process. When there is a significant ownership interest—say, a 20 to 40 percent share, however—the board had better take the call and listen to what they have to say.

At least two significant institutional shareholders agree with our view. Kenneth West, a senior consultant with TIAA CREF—which, with $240 billion, is the world's largest investment fund—also served on the NACD's (National Association of Corporate Directors) 1998 blue-ribbon panel on CEO succession. Succession, West states, must be a board-driven process: "One of the barriers to good succession is when boards let institutional shareholders become overly powerful in the process," he says. "There can definitely be inappropriate shareholder involvement. What's appropriate? When we see a case of clear underperformance on the part of the CEO, and the board isn't doing anything about it, we take action through the board."

Nell Minow, a principal of activist money manager LENS, which invests primarily in companies that are viewed as undervalued and not living up to their potential, agrees with West's assessment of the role of institutional shareholders. "Our job as shareholders," says Minow, "is to make sure the board does its job—not to do their job for them. When we were trying to ensure effective succession management at Waste Management, for example, we did communicate with the board. We asked questions like, 'How's succession going' and indicated qualifications we were looking for in a successor, but we would not tell them specifically who to talk to or precisely what to do."

While both of these institutional shareholders are aware of and seem to observe the proper boundaries when dealing with the board on succession issues, boards have to be vigilant about not letting any shareholder group gain control of the process. In short, these relationships must be carefully and diplomatically managed to provide adequate input, but not so much that the board's role and responsibility are undermined in any way.

Dealing with the Media—Whether You Like It or Not

The press can play a powerful role in succession planning. A few journalists who cover the corporate governance beat seem to have a real knack for getting people to talk about plans that have not yet publicly been announced. When we are dealing with a situation that involves delicate and precise timing, as we have discussed in previous chapters—readying a successor, sending the right signals that he or she is the chosen one, dealing with outside candidates whose confidentiality must be carefully guarded to protect their current positions, timing a transition—the wrong word in print about any one of these things can throw carefully laid plans completely off track.

When a succession is taking place at a high-profile public company—particularly if it is being played out under crisis conditions involving an underperforming CEO or one who is ill—you can bet that the media will take a keen interest in the drama and the key actors involved. Charged not merely with reporting the news, the press have increasingly taken on the role of investigating and exposing waste, inefficiency, and other concerns that may have an impact on shareholders. In that context, the growing interest in succession crises is hardly surprising since, as we have discussed on a number of occasions in this book, a poorly planned succession can throw a company and its management into severe turmoil and cause the stock price to plummet. And make no mistake about it: The challenge of dealing effectively with the press is not one that is likely to go away.

How can companies get smarter about dealing with the press? And how can they learn to make the relationship work so it fulfills a need on both sides? The first page of any press relations manual would likely reveal that rule one is to find a way to manage the flow of information. This is a critical task for companies, particularly when they are in crisis mode. "No comment"—unless it is truly the only appropriate response at a given time—is no longer the response of choice.

The bottom line is that if there is something of interest to readers and shareholders, someone is going to get the information—firsthand from company sources, or elsewhere—to write the story. Boards must operate on the assumption that the journalist is not going to go away. You cannot manage the process perfectly no matter what you do, but they will continue calling you, and you will have to face them on some level. You may think you can avoid answering your phone forever, but this person may still be responsible for writing a story, whether you cooperate or not, so you need to develop a strategy.

So one best practice is, when at all possible, to communicate openly and honestly. If a journalist has to rely on other than official company spokespeople, there is no telling what sort of an ax other individuals may have to grind and how the truth may be twisted. This may make matters much worse than if the company had merely responded to the original inquiry. The board should assume, particularly if it is a high-profile situation in which the public has a lot of interest, that details and circumstances surrounding the transactions are going to get out to the public domain. Therefore, the best course is for the responsible party, a representative of the search committee or a public relations representative, to share as much accurate information as possible so that journalists do not need to depend on less reliable sources.

Unfortunately, much of the sizzle reporters would like companies to provide—background on personalities, rivalries, and politics—is just the sort of information that could derail a successful succession. Much of what occurs during the process, as we have discussed, involves delicate timing and confidences that must be observed, whether companies are attempting to hold on to talent they have or to attract outstanding managers from the outside. It is often in the companies' best interest not to comment at all when in the midst of the search.

While she realizes it is somewhat in the realm of fantasy, Joann Lublin, of the *Wall Street Journal,* suggests an ongoing dialogue that would go something like this: "It would help if the company said, 'Okay, we've been at this two months now. We looked at twenty candidates initially, we knocked it down to five, and now we've got three who look like they're really top-notch and at some point we are going to have to decide between two candidates and hopefully we'll do that by December.'"

This sort of update between companies undergoing a transition at the top and the press is unlikely to take place. But companies may want to share what they can when they can with the press, particularly afterward, when some insight into a well-run succession may well serve the companies' interests.

"Board members may use the press as a trial board for their succession candidates," comments Joann Lublin. "While that can be somewhat explosive or difficult for the individuals involved, it really does get a shareholder reaction very quickly, as well as a response. . . . I think there is a lot that the company can get out of discussing some of these issues, by bringing them into the public arena. Obviously, you don't always control how that comes out, but if there are trusted relationships [between the journalist and the source] and people who understand what's going on in the company, it's potentially a very good way to bring some of these issues, that are so sensitive within the company, into the open, and then force people to discuss what it means if this person takes the role."

Surprisingly, some journalists do not give the press high marks for their succession coverage. Partially, they say, this is a result of their mandate to cover high-profile stories. This means less time to cover ongoing succession issues, especially those that are proceeding well, which, by their very nature, are simply not as interesting. "The problem," according to Jennifer Reingold of *Business Week,* "is that it's hard to get people to sit and talk with us during a well-planned, ongoing search. We did that succession cover story [August 1997] and spent a lot of time discussing succession with Campbell's Soup, where it was really well done. It's a struggle, though, because it's not as sexy as the one that blows up."

When companies do have information they are able to share, the company has to have a capable and well-informed spokesperson as well as a strategy for release. As far as a spokesperson, "experience is the best teacher," says Reingold. "My best sources and relationships at companies are with people who have been on lots of different boards—been there, done that. They aren't terrified of the media and they are savvy enough to know that publicity is not necessarily a negative thing—that it can work to the company's advantage."

One clear best practice is to have the chairman of the search committee be the spokesperson for the company vis-à-vis the outside world. This individual should be best positioned to make judgment calls about what the press should be told about the search as well as the timing for sharing information. Ideally, the search chairman should be a retired CEO who possesses not only the time but also the experience to deal with all the sensitivities, within and outside the company, entailed in the search.

The safest and fairest way to release information about the outcome of a search is to release it to everyone at once, at a time when all major publications will have a fair shot at using it. This, of course, means being aware of closing times at various publications, particularly those that are not dailies, but any capable press relations representative should have access to this information. The other alternative is to offer an exclusive to a particular publication. This approach can go a long way toward developing a good working relationship with a particular publication—perhaps different ones on different occasions—and may be the route to take if there is a particularly interesting issue involved in the succession that might merit a more intensive management story timed to appear at the same time as, or immediately after, the news story about a new CEO appointment.

As with all press relationships, corporate spokespeople must constantly and carefully consider any information to be shared; the interests of the press in covering the story are likely to be quite different from the interests of the company. By providing accurate and timely information on succession, whenever possible, companies can help ensure that an accurate message is conveyed to the public, including investors.

While not every company will be confronted with the full spectrum of scenarios explored in this chapter, most will have to deal with one or two at some point in a succession cycle. Of course, every company—especially higher-profile public companies—must learn to deal confidently with the press.

Board Checklist

We conclude this chapter with our board checklist, a reminder of things to be wary of when dealing with any of the "flashing yellow light" practices:

1. When it comes to mergers of equals, where all prior succession planning may suddenly become irrelevant, boards have to be vigilant to ask the right questions—particularly regarding how a possible power-sharing arrangement will work—before they consider approving a deal.

2. If a co-CEO arrangement is part of the deal, try to look beyond the initial period and devise a timetable for the transfer of power to a single CEO. This often works best when there is a younger CEO paired with an older counterpart who is approaching retirement.

3. Make sure the merger is being pursued for sound strategic reasons, not primarily to provide a successor, or a final blaze of glory, for the CEO.

4. While it is probably best not to have the former CEO remain on the board for more than a transitional period, if he or she does remain, it must be clear to the board who is leader of the company.

5. A company may choose to have a director step into the CEO role as a stopgap measure, rather than hire from outside, until the planned internal successor is better prepared. Under similar circumstances a director may serve as nonexecutive chairman. As with a co-CEO arrangement, these practices are best considered temporary solutions to be undertaken for a specified time.

6. A board managing a succession should have a search com-
    mittee to streamline the process, chaired by someone with
    adequate time and energy to organize necessary tasks,
    screen candidates, and deal with the press, among other
    responsibilities. A retired CEO is often the ideal board
    member to head the search committee.
7. Large institutional investors should be given the opportu-
    nity for input, but not the opportunity to wrest control of
    the succession process from the board.
8. Deal as openly as possible with the media. If you are able to
    provide timely, accurate information, they are less likely to
    tap less reliable—and more dangerous—second- and third-
    hand sources.

More than anything else, "flashing yellow light" practices provide a
means of managing change, or a way of dealing with circumstances a
company has not previously confronted. These practices can provide
effective solutions. If used properly, they can augment established best
practices, not subvert them. Back to best practices for a look at a distil-
lation of our recommendations in our next and final chapter.

10

Conclusion: Core Principles Yield Best Practices

Companies that have their priorities straight regarding roles and responsibilities for succession planning share a number of common best practices. Certainly very few companies would encompass every one of these recommended practices, but drawing from the best of the best, each of the following ten practices makes a statement about how succession is viewed and planned at companies that are serious about implementing and maintaining an effective succession planning process:

1. *They have strong, involved boards.* Companies that are effective in succession planning have boards that are deeply involved in the process with the CEO on an ongoing basis.
2. *They continually expose their top-management team to the board.* Companies that are effective in succession have CEOs who provide regular and meaningful business and social exposure of potential inside candidates to members of the board.
3. *They encourage "next-generation CEOs" to gain exposure to outside board service, to the media, and to the investment community.* Companies that are effective in succession provide opportunities to the top-tier executives to serve on a few outside boards and to be exposed to investment analysts

and other opinion makers on Wall Street and in the media. This helps to shape their understanding of the proper relationship between board and management, and the forces at work outside the company.

4. *They form executive committees or operating committees to facilitate the development of several executives who are aware of challenges, business plans, and strategies across the entire organization.* Companies that are effective in succession have CEOs who develop small teams of insiders who become "interchangeable" through cross-training and continuous exposure to the entire business.

5. *They view succession planning as an ongoing and "real time" process.* Companies that are effective in succession planning have boards and CEOs who communicate regularly (at least one or two times yearly) on a formal basis to determine who would likely be in line to take over in the event of a crisis. These discussions are linked to the strategic planning process to ensure a fit between where the business is going and the skills of the "next of kin."

6. *They take as much of the human drama out of the succession process as possible.* Companies that are effective in the succession process try to build in as much predictability concerning the outcome as possible. By openly communicating succession plans and timing to number twos, encouraging a team approach to the leadership of a corporation, and reducing "horse races" among top contenders, there is less risk of losing valuable top executives when the successor is named. It is also common to aggressively "handcuff" the top team to discourage defections when emotions run high before this critical period.

7. *They link the CEO's compensation to the development of succession plans.* Companies that are effective in succession have boards that require the CEO to report regularly on succession-planning activities with various contingency plans and formally link this to their bonus opportunity. Some corporations are beginning to attach a specific for-

mula (up to one-third of total bonus opportunity) based on their success in this area.

8. *They pay their directors increasingly in stock and require directors to make a personal investment in the company.* Some companies that are effective in succession are guided by a philosophy that directors take succession more seriously when their own economic interests are at stake. This is achieved, they argue, by requiring directors to purchase "significant" equity in the company.

9. *They periodically calibrate likely internal candidates for CEO against comparable outside leaders.* Companies that are successful in succession planning have systems in place to develop "market intelligence" on outside candidate possibilities on an ongoing basis to ensure that the best possible leader is tapped from the broadest possible universe. This process is especially important in those companies undergoing substantial change where outside experience may be critical to execute a new strategy or to change the momentum or direction of the business.

10. *They develop a "succession culture."* Companies that are effective in succession not only take CEO succession seriously but also have boards and CEOs who require all levels of the organization to plan for the inevitability of change. Some of these organizations have developed matrices for succession involving dozens of top executives and "high potentials" to ensure that they are given the proper tools, exposure, and training to develop into contenders for advancement.

We hope we have conveyed not merely the importance but also the urgency of tackling succession planning immediately, perhaps using these practices as a guide to action. We strongly believe that boards must act now or face the consequences sooner or later. It is all too easy to put off what appear to be nonimmediate concerns when everyday business concerns cry out for attention. But, because crises, by definition, strike without warning, we urge boards to help get their companies' house in order now. Proper planning on all the levels we have discussed means that boards will be forearmed and prepared to face the future—whatever it may be—with the confidence and the knowledge that they have done their best to protect the organizational and financial stability of their company.

Appendix

Quantifying the Trend
to Director Independence

To those who believe in the importance of directors possessing a proprietary mind-set—to be able to think like the owners they should be as well as those they represent—the trends in director compensation are positive. The Spencer Stuart Board Index (SSBI), data we have collected for the past fifteen years, indicates that a growing number of companies have been structuring board compensation so that directors are less beholden to the CEO: less like employees, more like owners. Along the same lines, forms of compensation that are usually considered employee benefits, such as retirement plans, are much less likely to apply to directors. In fact, they are rapidly being eliminated. In addition, compensation for directors is now much more inclined to reward performance for the long term rather than the short term, a trend that is similar to that for CEOs and other key executives.

- *Average Retainer Inches Up.* The average annual retainer for boards included in the SSBI ($43,540) rose 7 percent in 1999 over the previous year, but jumped a substantial 40 percent over five years ago. The distribution of the retainer, as well as the actual average, also has changed. While nearly one-fifth of SSBI companies paid retainers in the $20,000 to $24,000 range in 1994, by 1999 only a scant 5 percent of companies did. And while in 1994 no SSBI companies were represented in the highest category—$50,000 and up—by 1999 about a quarter of SSBI companies were.

- *Committee Meeting Fees Being Phased Out.* A look at the five-year trend in committee meeting fees demonstrates a slow but steady decline. Some 81 percent of companies included in our index paid such fees in 1994, a percentage that dropped to 71 percent in 1997, and dropped further to 66 percent in 1999. While there is a dramatic range in fees among those companies, the average committee meeting fee has remained virtually unchanged over the past five years, hovering at about $1,000.

- *Committee Retainers Dwindling as Well.* A shrinking number of companies are paying directors an individual retainer for serving on a committee. One-third of Stuart Spencer Board Index companies engaged in the practice in 1994; that had declined to just under one-quarter in 1998, including only about 15 percent of S&P 500 companies. At two-thirds of index companies the chairman still receives an individual committee retainer. At a small number of companies, retainers for both committee members and chairmen may vary by committee.

- *Huge Jump in "Stock Granted in Addition to Retainer."* As we have noted for the past several years, the variable element of stock and its fluctuating value figures more and more prominently in the compensation package of directors. A tiny but significant number of companies pay directors exclusively in stock. Though companies may elect one of several ways to compensate with stock, there is little question that encouraging equity on the part of directors is now considered a best practice by the majority of companies. Of particular note is the substantial increase in the number of companies that grant stock in addition to retainers: from 39 percent of SSBI companies in 1994 to more than half this year. There was also a dramatic increase in the number of companies that give directors a choice between cash compensation and equity: only one in ten among SSBI companies in 1994, and presently three out of four companies. Presumably—if directors do their jobs well—

the market should reward their efforts handsomely in the future.

- *Director Investment Required or Strongly Encouraged.* Increasingly, directors hold substantial equity in the companies on whose boards they serve. This has not happened by accident but rather is part of a deliberate policy on the part of many companies. In some cases, stock ownership by directors is compulsory, meaning that there is some indication in the proxy that the company requires, either explicitly or implicitly, directors to own shares. For our analysis "explicity stated" means the company specifies a number or dollar value of shares that directors must own; that they specify that deferred stock units to directors may not be sold until after retirement; or that directors are granted restricted stock units (which almost always means that they can't be sold until retirement). "Implicitly indicated" means that companies grant some form of deferred or phantom units and directors must hold onto an ongoing balance of such shares. In these cases it is not always possible to confirm that directors maintain equity. Where we could not confirm this, we did not count companies as among those requiring any form of stock ownership. It is interesting to note that a clear majority of responding SSBI companies (58%) maintain some sort of compulsory stock ownership policy for directors.

Recommended Reading

Bennis, Warren G., and David A. Heenan. *Co-Leaders: The Power of Great Partnerships.* New York: John Wiley & Sons, 1999.

Bowen, William W. *Inside the Boardroom: Governance by Directors and Trustees.* New York: John Wiley & Sons, 1994.

Collins, James C., Jerry I. Porras. *Built to Last.* New York: Harper-Collins, 1994.

General Motors. *Guidelines on Significant Corporate Governance Issues.* Detroit: General Motors, 1994.

National Association of Corporate Directors. *The Blue Ribbon Commission on Director Compensation.* Washington, D.C.: National Association of Corporate Directors, 1995.

——. *The Report of the Blue Ribbon Commission on CEO Succession.* Washington, D.C.: National Association of Corporate Directors, 1998.

Sonnenfeld, Jeffrey A. *The Hero's Farewell: What Happens When CEOs Retire.* New York: Oxford University Press, 1988.

Index